Anne R. Gladstone Bennett

Einsiedeln in the dark wood

Our Lady of the hermits: the story of an alpine sanctuary

Anne R. Gladstone Bennett

Einsiedeln in the dark wood
Our Lady of the hermits: the story of an alpine sanctuary

ISBN/EAN: 9783741139246

Manufactured in Europe, USA, Canada, Australia, Japa

Cover: Foto ©Thomas Meinert / pixelio.de

Manufactured and distributed by brebook publishing software
(www.brebook.com)

Anne R. Gladstone Bennett

Einsiedeln in the dark wood

Einsiedeln «in the dark wood».

————

Einsiedeln.

EINSIEDELN

„IN THE DARK WOOD"

OR

OUR LADY OF THE HERMITS.

THE STORY OF AN ALPINE SANCTUARY.

WITH NUMEROUS ILLUSTRATIONS.

——— ■ ———

EINSIEDELN, SWITZERLAND,
NEW-YORK, CINCINNATI & ST. LOUIS
CHARLES & NICHOLAS BENZIGER BROTHERS.

———

LONDON: BURNS AND OATES.
1883.

PREFACE

THE account given in the following pages of the Shrine of our Lady of the Hermits and of the Monastery at Einsiedeln has been in a great measure compiled and translated from a most able and exceedingly interesting little work in German which has recently been published by Messrs. Benziger under the title of,

Beschreibung des Klosters und der Wallfahrt.

Extracts have also been made from a very learned work by *Rev. Fr Albert Kuhn* on Einsiedeln, now in course of publication, and from a French guide-book bearing the title of *Précis historique de l'abbaye et du pèlerinage de Notre-Dame-des-Ermites.*

The concluding portion is devoted to the personal recollections of a visit made by me to Einsiedeln during the summer of 1881.

TOURS, March 1882.

ANNE R. BENNETT
née GLADSTONE.

**greeting to the Blessed Virgin Mary of Einsiedeln,
translated from the German.**

———

All hail to thee, rich source of every grace!
Oh! Throne of graces of the Queen of Heaven!
With childlike trust I near the holy place
Where graces numberless for pilgrims flow;
Where breathes within the lovely Alpine vale
Sweet calm and rest and God's own holy peace.
Hark! Mary calls, oh come, all ye who wail
And who are weary, come, from tumult rest.
The burdens pressing on you lay down here;
Pour out your hearts before your Mother! See
With Mother's eyes she greets her children dear.
Come linger trustfully within her house.
Oh Mother! let the peace of this sweet vale
Flow also thro' my poor and storm-tossed soul;
And let me also henceforth never fail
As well thy servant as thy child to be.

———

Chapter i.

St. Meinrad.

Amongst the many thousands of tourists who year after year visit the „play-ground" of Europe, ascending its snow-capped mountains and exploring the recesses of its picturesque Alpine vallies, how few there are, at any rate of the English-speaking peoples, who are aware that Switzerland has something far more beautiful and more grand to ˙shew them than even its glaciers and its majestic mountains. Here and there, indeed, some chance traveller may be found, who, having heard of the Sanctuary „in the dark wood" has turned his steps thither. But even he, when he has reached the goal of his pilgrimage, seldom remains longer than a couplé of days at Einsiedeln and therefore, takes away with him but a very faint and incomplete idea of a place which would have made him feel himself to be transported back to the ages of faith. It was my happy lot to spend two months

last year at the Shrine of Our Lady of the
Hermits, and it seems to me that an account of
Einsiedeln, the Monastery, the Church, and the
Pilgrimage thither, cannot fail to interest and to
attract many to make a visit to a spot consecra-
ted by the blood of St. Meinrad and the Divine
Dedication of the Church built over his cell.

It is from Wädensweil, a quaint little village
situated on the charming shores of the Lake of
Zurich, on whose waters, hundreds of little vessels
ply from side to side, that the pilgrim wends his
way to Einsiedeln by means of the Wädensweil
mountain railway. As he reaches higher ground,
the view of the Lake becomes more and more
delightful, its smiling banks being dotted with
villas and farmhouses, each of them surrounded
by orchards or vineyards, whilst lofty heights
bound the horizon. Far away below, on the
shining waters, his eyes rest with pleasure upon
the pretty little island of Ufnau and its ancient
church; and in the distance, he catches a
glimpse of the island of Lutzelau and the lofty
and majestic towers of Rapperschwyl with its
dam stretching like a dark ribbon across the
lake. The chief object of merit in the little town
is the possession of the Great Polish National
Museum, containing very many objects of great
historical interest. Strangers are freely admitted

Wädensweil on the Lake of Zurich.

to view the collection, which is the only one in Switzerland, and one of the finest of its kind.

Arrived at Schindellegi, he will find that the road crosses the Sihl, a picturesque mountain torrent, which flows into the Lake of Zurich, and that he has exchanged his outlook over the Lake for one in which the more austere characteristics of an Alpine valley are predominant. Passing by St. Meinrad's Brunnen he will next reach Biberbruck and crossing the Alp will see stretched out before him the green pastures of the secluded valley of Einsiedeln.

Before giving a detailed description of a place which may indeed he called „the House of God and the Gate of Heaven" it will be well to cast a glance over the history of St. Meinrad, as it has been handed down to us in the old chronicles and manuscripts preserved in the Benedictine Monastery at Einsiedeln.

According to the oldest records extant, St. Meinrad, to whom the Sanctuary „in the dark wood" owes its origin, sprang from the noble race of the Hohenzollern, and was born at Sulchen, the Castle of his maternal ancestors, about the year 797. During his infancy, his mother, a woman of lofty mind and cultivated intellect, superintended his education and whilst still a child he acquired under her influence manners singularly marked by calmness and modesty; his physiognomy bearing the impress of a gravity, which, even in his tender years commanded respect. As soon as the boy had attained the requisite age, his father, Count Berchtold, sent him to the then famous school attached to the Abbey of Reichenau, situated on an island bearing the same name on the Lake of Constance. Two of Meinrad's relatives were established there, one of them being the Abbot Hatto by name, the other, the Monk Erlebad, who was one of the most distinguished and cultivated men of his time. The Abbot having been raised to the Episcopal see of Bâle, Erlebad was appointed Abbot in his place; but his elevation did not prevent him from superintending, as assiduously as before, the education of his nephew. Meinrad, under such careful tuition, soon became as learned as his masters, without on that account losing his modest simplicity of manner. More than once, while giving lessons to his nephew, Erlebad was struck with admiration and astonishment and predicted for him a glorious future in the Monastery over which he himself presided. When, however, he spoke on the subject to the youth, whose heart was already filled with longings for the religious life, Meinrad would not give a decisive answer, saying he must first consult his father. Having done so the Count replied that he felt he should he wanting in his duty to God if he were to combat his son's desire, and accordingly Meinrad assumed the Benedictine habit in the year 822, and the 25th year of his age. A little later on he was sent as a teacher to Bollingen on the upper Lake of Zurich, where the Benedictines of Reichenau had established a school. But the view that he always had before him there of the forest-clad summits of the Etzel, rising from the opposite side of the lake, excited in the heart of the pious young man more and more ardent longings for a wholly solitary life. At last, having seriously weighed the question, Meinrad, with the permission of his Superiors betook himself to the heights of the Etzel, in the year 828, there to lead the life of a hermit.

A holy widow of Altendorf having given him permission, he built for himself a little oratory, and close beside it a cell, where he lived, and where the pious woman came day by day to supply him with the necessaries of life.

But Meinrad was not allowed to remain long in quiet enjoyment of his beloved solitude. From far and near, crowds soon began to resort to the saintly hermit for counsel and conference on spiritual matters. So, after having spent seven years on the Etzel, he fled away from his cell and withdrew still farther into the depths of the „dark wood."

It was upon a small table-land, the south side of which was protected by a hill enclosing it like an amphitheatre, and close to a clear bright spring of water that Meinrad at last established himself and, with the permission of the Abbess Hedwig, built himself a dwelling and a Chapel which was destined in after times to develope into the famous Benedictine monastery and pilgrimage Church of Einsiedeln. His only possessions were the rule of St. Benedict, a missal, a book of homilies, the works of the Monk Cassian and the statue of the Blessed Virgin, presented to him by the Abbess Hildegarde, a daughter of King Ludwig, which under the title of Our Lady of the Hermits is still the object of veneration in the holy chapel at Einsiedeln.

Meinrad had there passed many years of a life devoted to God and to his fellow creatures, when one unhappy day two robbers broke into his poor dwelling in the hopes of finding concealed treasure and the holy man at once recognising them as destined, in the counsels of the Most High, to be his murderers, gave them kindly welcome. But after he had supplied their needs, fed them at his table and given them warnings and advice how to provide for their own security, the two wicked men fell upon him, and slew him on the 21st of

January 861, the saint having lived at Einsiedeln
five and twenty years.

Hoping to find safety in flight, the murderers
betook themselves to Zurich, but were pursued
by two ravens belonging to the Saint. This un-
usual circumstance attracting the notice of the
people of Zurich, a carpenter of Wollerau hastened
to the cell of the Saint, and there discovered his
corpse, then returning to Zurich he made diligent
search for the murderers and having found them
he delivered them into the hands of the judge
by whom they were tried and condemned to death.

As soon as the tidings of this terrible murder
reached Reichenau, the Abbot Walter, accompanied by several of his Monks, set out for
St. Meinrad's cell „in the dark wood", and after
having deposited his heart on the summit of the
Etzel, he conveyed the rest of his mortal remains
to the Abbey of Reichenau in solemn procession.
For the space of 178 years the body of the Saint
remained there.

In the meantime, out of the little cell of
St. Meinrad, rose the vast Convent of Einsiedeln
and in the year 1039 the body of the Saint was
brought back to its cell where it is venerated
at the present day.

Amongst the old chronicles and manuscripts
preserved in the Convent of Einsiedeln is a very

interesting book profusely adorned with illustrations which most probably dates as far back as 1482. It was most likely intended as a souvenir for the pilgrims visiting Einsiedeln to whom it would serve as a precious remembrance of the days they had passed near St. Meinrad's tomb. As to the place where it was printed and the name of the author, nothing certain is known, tho' there seems a possibility that it may be ascribed to Albrecht von Bonstetten who wrote the legend of St. Idda and the life of Brother Klaus and who travelled to Italy to obtain from Pope Pius II., the ratification of the privileges bestowed at an earlier date on the Convent of Einsiedeln.

With regard to the contents of this most interesting book, of which only two copies are known to exist, they are, as may readily be imagined, most naïve in character and specially adapted to the popular taste. This is peculiarly observable in the woodcuts representing the murder of St. Meinrad which is given with all possible detail and in the most realistic manner. As is but natural, manners and customs characteristic of the fifteenth century are cast back into the ninth and particulars borrowed from the lives of other saints are introduced into the legend. A facsimile of this quaint old book was published in 1861, being the thousandth anniversary of St. Meinrad's death. A slight description of some of the illustrations can hardly fail to be of interest; at any rate the reader will thereby be enabled to place the saint before him as he appeared to the eyes of the readers of the legend nearly four hundred years ago.

The first of these rude, but bold and life-like illustrations, shows us Count Berchtold of Hohen-zollern praying to God for a son and promising that, if his request were granted, the child should be dedicated to His service. „God our Father," he exclaims, „I implore Thee, give me a child"; and an angel appearing to him in a cloud replies: „That which thou hast prayed for shall be granted to thee." In the following picture the Count is represented standing by the bed-side of his wife, with the child, which God had given him in his arms.

Then, in regular order, are given illustrations of Meinrad's career, showing how, after having received his early education, he is sent to Rei-chenau where we see him saying his first Mass and shortly after receiving a summons from the Abbot of Bollingen to betake himself thither. The surprise with which the humble saint receives the command and the simplicity with which he sets forth at once to obey it are most vividly depicted.

In the following illustration he is seen taking his departure from Bollingen accompanied by three of his scholars, who are a head and shoulders shorter than himself, and crossing the Lake of Zurich in a wide flat-bottomed boat; his countenance beaming with joy and his companions gazing at him with admiration. Having landed at the foot of the Etzel mountain they bend their steps towards the forest in search of a place wherein to take up their abode. After a while, Meinrad meets with a widow woman of whom he enquires whether he and his companions may remain in the „dark wood“, to which she replies „You and your young men are welcome“. In the following illustration she is represented as supplying the saint and his disciples with garments of which they seem in great need.

For the space of three days the two young men fish in a brook, which flows through the forest in a very impossible manner, while St. Meinrad, after having held converse with the widow woman, seeks for a still more solitary retreat wherein to spend his days. Hardly has he found one when a nest with two young ravens is brought to him by one of his disciples, or „little brothers“ (Bruderlin) as they are affectionately called. Then the three return to the widow's house where they are seen seated at a table partaking of fish and

bread, a further supply of fish frying the while
on a gridiron placed on the floor.

The meal ended, St. Meinrad departs for his
hermitage and his „little brothers" return to their
convent.

The next illustration shows us St. Meinrad
hard at work, surrounded by heaps of stones
and mortar, building his Chapel, whilst, on either
side of the altar are perched the two ravens with
outstretched necks and open beaks croaking their
satisfaction. But St. Meinrad is not allowed long
to remain at peace in his solitude and accordingly
we see him assaulted, whilst at his prayers before
the door of his cell, by two devils of frightful
aspect who beat him sorely with their heavy clubs.
But an angel comes to his rescue, and the ravens
settling on the heads of the devils peck them so
fiercely that they are obliged to take flight. Nor
is the Saint left without earthly friends, for the
widow with whom he had made acquaintance on
the Etzel visits him at Einsiedeln, bringing with
her fish in a basin wherewith to supply his
frugal wants.

Pilgrims also visit him frequently and we are
shown two of them approaching St. Meinrad's
cell and receiving at the hands of the Saint loaves
of bread and a cup of wine, a spectacle which
seems greatly to rejoice the ravens who are look-

Biberbrück near Einsiedeln.

ing down on the scene trom the gable where
they are perched on either side of a crucifix.

But all are not true pilgrims who resort to
St. Meinrad's cell, for the following illustration
shows us the robbers and murderers who have
been attracted thither by the fame of the charity
of the holy man and by the expectation of finding treasures of gold and silver concealed in
his hut. So they come and ask for food and
alms from the Saint who, seating them at his
table sets bread and wine before them, begging
them to tarry a while with him, but saying at the
same time „That for which you are come hither,do".
Even while they are eating bread and drinking
wine, the ravens, full of righteous indignation
settle on the heads of the murderers who, however
seem utterly insensible to their screams and the
vicious pecks which they inflict upon them. Hardly
have they ended their meal, when full of haste to
carry out their evil designs they set upon the
Saint and beat him with clubs, the one saying to
the other „let me kill the Monk, thou canst not
do it" and all the time the ravens are pecking
their foreheads, till at last death comes to relieve
the Saint from his sufferings.

Then suddenly, so we are told, the forest is
filled with a sweet odour, and the murderers,
perhaps seized with remorse, lay St. Meinrad out,

placing a ca.. ile at his head and another at his
feet, whilst an angel coming down from heaven
lights them with a flaming torch which he holds
in his hand. On seeing this the murderers take
flight, and at the very same moment a carpenter,
a friend of St. Meinrad's, hewing wood at the door
of his house says suddenly to his brother that
he fears some harm has happened to the Saint
and he will set out to seek him. In the following illustration the carpenter and his brother,
their friends and relations and acquaintances are
gathered together and are seen weeping over
the body of St. Meinrad; then they hasten back
to Zurich where the two murderers, pursued by
the ravens, have already betaken themselves. The
criminals, being discovered by the screams and
croaking of the ravens, are quickly seized and
brought before the Burgomaster who, finding in
the birds sufficient testimony of „Peter's" and
„Richard's" guilt, sentences them to be tied with
ropes to a horse and dragged over sharp rocks;
the ravens meantime tearing their naked flesh
and continuing to cling to them, when they are
bound to wheels and afterwards set on piles over
a fire, the flames of which speedily consume them.
The lives of both of them being thus miserably
ended, their ashes are cast into a running stream as
being unworthy of christian burial. In the fol-

lowing illustration we are shown St. Meinrad's
corpse, conveyed on a bier drawn by oxen from
Einsiedeln up the Etzel and placed in the Chapel
which, from that day forward, has been known
by his nàme.

The next picture portrays the removal of
St. Meinrad's remains to Reichenau where the
Abbot, clad in cope and mitre, preceded by his
cross-bearer, and accompanied by a monk, carrying his crosier, goes forth to meet them. With
this illustration the series representing the history
of St. Meinrad concludes.

There still remain a few more woodcuts to
be described. The first of these shows us our
Lady's Chapel in the „dark wood" falling into
ruins and almost buried beneath the forest-trees
and rank herbage which have sprung up around
it. The next exhibits St. Gregory preaching at
Rome during the year of the Jubilee and asking
whether any one amongst his audience can tell
him where the „dark wood" in Germany is situated; to which question a monk replies in the
affirmative, whilst an angel descends bearing with
him a scroll whereon are inscribed the words
„Thou shalt go to the dark wood".

St. Eberhard, praying in his church at Stras-
burg, also receives from an angel a similar command bidding him go to „the dark wood" and

betake himself to the Chapel of Our Lady of
the Hermits.

In the following woodcut we see St. Gregory
toiling up the mountain of the Etzel accompanied
by a „Brother" from Zurich who pointing upwards with his finger says to the Saint: „This is
the dark wood", *„Das ist der finstere Wald"*.

There St. Gregory meets St. Eberhard and
after discoursing together respecting the command
laid upon them by God, they build up with their
own hands St. Meinrad's Chapel.

Only two more illustrations remain to be
mentioned. The first of these represents Our
Saviour and his angels consecrating the Chapel of
St. Meinrad and also shows us St. Conrad, Bishop
of Constance, being withheld from performing the
like sacred ceremony by the voice of an angel
speaking from heaven and saying „Cease Brother"
or as it is given in the legend borne in his hand
„Cessa frater".

The last illustration represents St. Conrad and
other holy men prostrate at the feet of the Pope
begging him to ratify the Divine Dedication. The
Bull granted by Pope Leo is then alluded to, but
as its contents had already been given to the world
the author does not repeat them in full and contents himself with concluding his work by an eloquent and beautiful greeting to Our Blessed Lady.

A very curious and striking frontispiece is attached to this most interesting old book, its subject being the Divine Dedication of the Chapel of St. Meinrad; it bears the date 1466. The tenderness of feeling and delicacy of execution which mark the original are clearly discernible in the fac-simile, proving the work to be that of a master. As to the meaning of the engraving there can be no doubt, seeing that it bears the following inscription: „This is the Divine Consecration of our dear Lady at Einsiedeln. Ave gratia plena!“ The Statue of the Blessed Virgin which is represented standing upon the altar closely resembles the one in the Holy Chapel. In a gallery above the altar the Son of God is seen sprinkling the sacred precincts with holy water, and in a line with Him God the Father, one hand raised in the act of blessing, the other resting on a book; on either side stand choirs of angels, some with musical instruments in their hands, whilst above the Holy Spirit is shown under the form of a dove.

As to the master (Meister E), whose initial is affixed to the engraving, many conjectures have been hazarded which are all equally unsatisfactory. It seems probable that he was the head of a school and that his pupils produced, with more or less of success, works in the same style as those which came from the hand of the master.

CHAPTER II.

The Monastery of Einsiedeln.

In the year 838, St. Meinrad took leave of his cell on the heights of the Etzel and withdrew still farther into the depths of the „dark wood" near the Sihl, where he built a little Chapel and a cell beside a spring of water. This was the commencement of the Convent of Einsiedeln.

In the year 1704, on the 31st of March, at five o' clock in the morning the Abbot Maurus von Roll accompanied by certain of his Monks, went forth from the Convent which up to that time he had inhabited and turned up the soil three times with his spade, as did also those that were with him; then the workmen advanced and began to dig the foundations on which the present Convent was destined to rise. Between the building of the first cell and of the Chapel of Our Blessed Lady by St. Meinrad and the great work undertaken by the forty-third Prince Abbot, nine centuries had elapsed, during which period Einsiedeln had been subjected to the vicissitudes which we shall now proceed to relate.

Seventy four years after St. Meinrad's death, St. Benno, a scion of a princely Burgundian house and a Canon of the Cathedral of Strasbourg, being inspired by Divine Grace, betook himself to the Hermitage of St. Meinrad accompanied by some of his friends of like mind. Arrived at their destination, they built cells for themselves which encircled the holy Chapel, and by their holy sacrifices, prayers and penances they illumined the „dark wood".

There St. Benno lived till 925, when he was elevated to the see of Metz. But his zeal in fulfilling his episcopal duties inflamed the minds of wicked men against him, and at last their malice rose to such a height that they dragged him from his Palace, tore out his eyes and drove him from his see. The King of Germany put to death the authors of this abominable crime and invited the holy prelate to return to his Diocese. But St. Benno preferred to go back to his beloved cell and the companions he had left there and among them he died the death of the just in the year 940.

St. Benno was still living when another dignitary of the Cathedral of Strasbourg, Eberhard

The Monastery.

3

by name, a member of a noble French family,
decided to follow his example.   In the autumn
of the year 934, he arrived with a very numerous
suite at St. Meinrad's Hermitage and, soon
after his coming there, drew the plan of a church
and a large monastery to be built on the spot
consecrated by St. Meinrad's blood. The Chapel
of the Saint dedicated to the Mother of God and
already the goal of many pilgrimages was to remain on the site which it had always occupied,
whilst around and above it were to rise the walls
and roof of the Church.   In every succeeding
reconstruction of the Monastery these features
were retained. The Monastery was finished in 946
and, two years later, the Church. That was the
first Monastery at Einsiedeln. We have but little
information respecting the aspect of the building,
but the ecclesiastical architecture of that early
period was so severe and simple in its character
that it is not difficult to form an idea of the
appearance presented by the Church which must
have been a flat-roofed Basilica of the usual
oblong form, and the Monastery an irregular pile
of buildings devoid of any special beauty.

St. Eberhard, by means of his great wealth,
and the aid afforded him by neighbouring lords,
having built the Monastery, was elected first
Abbot of the Community and gave to his Monks

the rule of St. Benedict placing the Convent beneath the protection of the Blessed Virgin under the title of Our Lady of the Hermits. He then begged of Conrad, Bishop of Constance, to consecrate the Holy Chapel and also the Church attached to the Monastery. It was on the eve of the 14th of September 948, that the venerable Bishop arrived at Einsiedeln, together with the holy Bishop of Augsburg and a great number of knights and gentlemen. On that same eve the Bishop rose, according to his wont, at midnight and went to the Church to pray in the Holy Chapel, accompanied by some of the monks. He had been there but a short time when suddenly it was filled with light brighter than that of the sun at midday, while the chanting of psalms by a great multitude fell upon his ears. Hastening towards the altar which was illuminated as for a solemn festival he beheld, standing in front of the statue of Our Blessed Lady, Jesus Christ Himself assisted by the four Evangelists, offering up the Most Holy Sacrifice; Angels standing on either side of the Divine Pontiff wafted incense on the air, the Apostles SS. Peter and Paul and the Pope St. Gregory bore in their hands the Pontifical insignia. A choir of angels made the Church resound with their celestial songs and SS. Stephen and Laurence officiated as deacons.

St. Conrad himself relates in his book, *de secretis secretorum* that the text of the Sanctus was thus modified by the angelic voices; *Sanctus Deus in aula gloriosæ Virginis, miserere nobis! Benedictus Mariæ filius in æternum regnaturus qui venit!* He also cites variations in the Agnus as well as in the blessing which ran thus „May the blessing of Heaven rest upon you, and may the angels, may God Himself make His dwelling in you."

Astonished though he was by such a celestial apparition, the Bishop did not at once leave the Holy Chapel, but continued to pray there till the eleventh hour of the morning. At last, not having made his appearance, the monks who had been long awaiting his return went into the Church to beg that he would perform the ceremony which had been fixed to take place on that day. He then related to them what he had seen and refused to consecrate a chapel which had already received a Divine Dedication. No one, however, gave credence to his recital, on the contrary, he was harshly blamed by St. Eberhard and ordered at once to begin the ceremonial. Accordingly, after having made long resistance to the utmost of his power, the Bishop withdrew his opposition, and, returning to the Church prepared to ascend the steps of the altar in the holy Chapel in the presence of a great concourse of people who had

The Miraculous Consecration.

collected together from all parts. But no sooner
had his foot reached the first step of the altar,
than a voice, heard by all present, and which
seemed to descend from heaven, exclaimed „Cease,
brother, the Chapel is divinely consecrated".
— „*Cessa, cessa, frater, Capella divinitus conse-
crata est.*"

This marvellous history was afterwards confirmed by numerous contemporary witnesses, by
judicial enquiries signed by the highest civil and
ecclesiastical authorities and lastly, sixteen years
later, by a bull of Pope Leo VIII, given at the
instance and in the presence of St. Conrad, of
the Emperor Otto, of his spouse Adelheid and ·
of many other personages, secular and ecclesiastic,
assembled together at the foot of the apostolic
throne. ·After relating the particulars of the Divine Consecration the bull pronounces an ana-
thema upon any who, in the future, should dare
to renew the consecration of the Holy Chapel,
and concludes with these words: „We absolve all
who shall visit the above-named holy spot, after
confession and repentance, from all their sins and
the penalties attached thereto.

This bull was confirmed by Pope Innocent IV.
and many succeeding Pontiffs, among whom may
be named Leo X. and Clement VII. Pius VI.
ratified the bulls of his predecessors on the

15th of May 1773, „to honour the Monastery, and to shame sceptics, who are always ready to cast doubts upon events which it does not suit them to believe and to place implicit faith in any absurdities which please their taste."

The Monastery built by St. Eberhard did not last even a hundred years. In 1029, according to an old chronicler, a miserable knight, Eppo von Stetten by name, a wretch hated of God and man, burnt the House of God at Einsiedeln down to the ground. The Holy Chapel, however, remained uninjured in the midst of the desolation, but the whole of the monastery fell a prey to the flames.

In the year 1031, Embrich, the fifth Prince Abbot, laid the foundation stone of another Church and Monastery, which was completed in 1039. That same year the new Convent and Church were solemnly consecrated, with the exception, of course, of the Holy Chapel, by the Bishop of Constance and, on that occasion also, the remains of St. Meinrad were brought back from Reichenau to the Chapel in the dark wood. No further information respecting the second Monastery of Einsiedeln has been handed down to us.

Two centuries passed by and then another conflagration took place, with regard to which some chroniclers state that the Church only was burnt to the ground, whilst others assert that the Monastery shared the same fate. But all agree in affirming that the Chapel of the Mother of God, although built almost entirely of wood, was miraculously spared.

It was Conrad I, Count of Thun, at that time reigning as Prince Abbot, who undertook the building of the third Monastery, which, as soon as it was brought to completion, was consecrated by the Bishop of Constance.

During two hundred and forty one years the Convent remained uninjured. In 1467, however, the Church fell once more a prey to the flames. On Quasimodo Sunday everything in the sacred building that was constructed of wood, together with all the ornaments, chalices and books were destroyed, „only" the old chronicler adds, „the Holy Chapel suffered no harm notwithstanding that much wood had been employed in the construction of its walls".

From other sources we learn that a portion of the Monastery also was destroyed by the flames which had attacked the Church and therefore a fourth reconstruction of the building became necessary. It was then that the Chapel of Our Lady was rebuilt with hewn stones and vaulted over.

But before it was possible to carry out the plans which had been drawn for the extension of the Monastery, a fire broke out on the 30th of

March 1509, in a cottage, and spreading to the
village consumed it entirely, damaging also a portion of the Church and part of the Monastery;
the Holy Chapel, as on every former occasion,
being miraculously preserved from harm. As soon
as the conflagration had reached the Monastery,
Abbot Conrad hastened to the „Chapel where, in
the words of the historian, he prayed very earnestly and piously to God and at the conclusion
of his prayer, being filled with great zeal and
confidence in the Mother of God, he exclaimed,
„Oh Mary, Mother of God, take heed, for all that
is here is thine and belongs wholly to thee."
Then he went forth from the Chapel and said
he knew positively that the fire would not come
near the Abbot's house, which prediction came
to pass, for it remained untouched by the flames."

The injuries which the Church and Convent
received on this occasion were not, happily, of
a nature to render necessary their entire reconstruction. Between the years 1544 and 1569 a
cupola was placed above the Holy Chapel and
we are also informed that this fourth Monastery
was more regular and beautiful in style than had
been the former buildings.

The majestic construction had now attained
the height of its splendour, it had been restored at
vast cost and nothing was wanting to its magni-

ficence; all on which the eye rested was grand
and beautiful as became the House of God.

But Ecce! in the ninth year of the reign of
the Prince Abbot Adam Heer, a fearful raging
fire broke out again in the village, and burnt
down, not only all the houses therein, but also
the Monastery, together with the Church and all
the ornaments it contained, doing no injury however to the Holy Chapel. This terrific conflagration began about noon on St. Mark's day 1577.
It lasted three or four hours only, but in that short
space of time everything that was not conveyed
out of doors was utterly destroyed. All the roofs
of the houses in the village, as well as that of the
Monastery, were covered either with tiles or shingles
and a fearful rushing wind drove the flames from
one house to another. Even to the Waggithal,
three long hours distant from Einsiedeln and separated from it by a mountain, half consumed
shingles and sheets of paper were carried by the
wind. The Prince Abbot chanced on that day to
be at the Convent of the Nuns at Au, about half
an hour distant from Einsiedeln, but on receiving
the terrible tidings he hastened to return in the
morning to the Monastery and has left in his own
handwriting a very touching description of the
desolation he found there. The Monastery was
entirely destroyed and became a mass of ruins,

the roof of the Church was consumed, the lofty cupola surmounting the towers had disappeared, all the bells had melted, even the stone work was injured, and the roof had great rents in it. But the destructive element had spent itself on the exterior of the building and scarcely any injury had been done to the interior though traces remained of the fiery tongues which had penetrated into it by roof and window.

But alas! all the works of art and the valuables collected in the newly - built treasure chambers and in other parts of the Monastery were utterly and irretrievably destroyed.

The building of the fifth Monastery was immediately undertaken by the Prince Abbot Adam, and finished by his successor Ulrich III. The new Monastery resembled its predecessor in all respects with the exception of some unimportant modifications.

The Convent and Church preserved the same aspect in all their essential details until the construction of the Choir and Penitentiary in the year 1674. It must, nevertheless be mentioned, that under the reign of every succeeding Abbot improvements were continually being effected.

That the Monastery was very hastily and badly built after the great fire of 1577 is clearly proved by the fact that after a lapse of fifty years

it was thought that it would be necessary to re-
build it. The intention was not, however, carried
out, and it is well that it was not, as the plans
which were designed in 1704 were in most respects much more grandiose than those of 1633.

It was in the year 1721 that Abbot Schenklin
of Wyl laid the foundation stone of the present
Church, which was solemnly consecrated in the
year 1735. The building of the Monastery, the
arcades and the flight of steps leading up from the
„Place" to the space in front of the Church, were
brought to a conclusion some years afterwards.

On the 1st November 1755 such terrible con-
vulsions of nature occurred that it was feared the
efforts made to beautify Einsiedeln would prove
vain. In an account given by an eye-witness we
are told that a few days after the earthquakes which
had taken place in Spain and Portugal, a fearful shaking to and fro of the earth was experienced
at the Monastery of Einsiedeln and every one
expected that the Church and the Choir would
fall in. It lasted about four minutes and many
persons being gathered together in the Choir for
Vespers they all fled away with pale faces and
could hardly persuade themselves to return.

Nothing was really injured, only an old crack
which had already been noticed in the Church
was widened. „God preserve us in future," con-

The Madonna of Einsiedeln.

cludes the pious writer „from all such-like visi-
tations," as indeed He has done up to the present day.

It was in the same year 1755 that on the
31st August the Prince Abbot Nicholas solemnly
consecrated the altar of the Rosary. The other
numerous altars were finished afterwards and
consecrated together with all the other buildings
forming portions of the Church, which had been
raised at the cost of so much time and trouble.
It is easy to understand why the diarist, after
giving these details, should associate with them
the wish that „all being brought to a conclusion
the happy hope may be entertained that the
Church will in future enjoy rest and that silence
may follcw the noise and turmoil of its building".

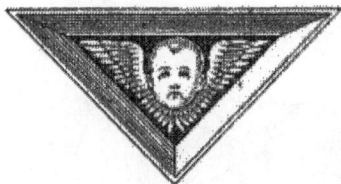

CHAPTER III.

The present Monastery.

THE pile of buildings of which the present Monastery is composed covers a space of 150 yards in width by 172 yards in length, the Church occupying the central portion of the principal façade. On either side are wings which are connected together by four pavilions placed at the north, south, east and west angles of the Monastery and which enclose within their walls four courts or gardens. The Monastery is two stories in height, exclusive of the ground floor, each story containing forty two windows. The pavilions at the angles are one story higher than the wings and add great dignity to the simple and severe style of the edifice. The interior is divided into four separate portions comprising, 1st the chambers of the Abbot, 2dly the apartments of the Monks, 3dly the College, 4thly the Library.

The suites of rooms occupied by the Abbot are situated in the pavilion and wing which look

towards the south. Stretching along one side of
the corridor are the guest chambers, and opposite
them the dining room and reception rooms. With
these last is connected a hall of noble proportions
decorated in the same style as the rest of the
Monastery, the ceiling being adorned with a fresco
by Deschwanden, representing the Divine Dedication of the Holy Chapel. On the walls hang
full length portraits of the Pope, the Emperors
of France, Germany and Austria and of some other
princely personages. In presenting their portraits
to the Monastery the most distinguished members of the royal families of Europe showed their
wish to perpetuate the relations which in former
times subsisted between them and the Convent,
as well as their sense of the services rendered
to them by the Benedictine Fathers in by-gone
ages. At the lower end of the great hall, which
is 33 yards long and wide in proportion, are two
large historical pictures given to the Monastery
on the occasion of the millenary festival in 1861,
by the Prince of Hohenzollern Sigmaringen. The
subject of one of these paintings is St. Meinrad
preaching on the Etzel; the figures grouped around
him being relations of the Prince whose ancestors
were nearly connected with the Saint. The pendant
represents the gift of the miraculous statue made
by the Abbess of Frauen Münster to St. Meinrad;

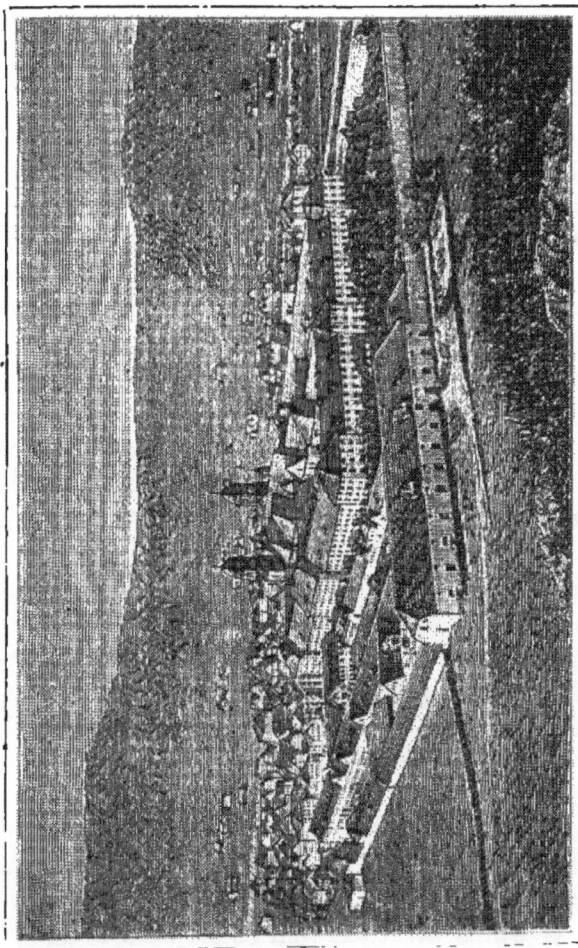

Bird's-eye-view of the Monastery from the East.

4

the four sons of the Prince occupying the most prominent positions in the composition.

Near these pictures is one of the Holy Father which Pope Pius IX of sacred memory bestowed on the Monastery as a mark of his sympathy on the occasion of the Jubilee. Then follow life-size portraits of the Emperor and Empress of Austria; of Louis Napoleon III and of the Empress Eugenie, also a very interesting drawing of the Prince Imperial taken when he was a child. Next in order is an excellent portrait of Frederic William IV, King of Prussia, who, as chief of the Hohenzollerns presented it to the Convent on the occasion of the Jubilee of his ancestor St. Meinrad, in 1861. In the year 1865 his brother, the present Emperor, sent his portrait to Einsiedeln and lastly, the Crown Princes of Austria and Prussia have testified their high estimation of the Monastery by also sending their portraits to adorn the hall.

Amongst the religious pictures may be mentioned a portrait of Brother Klaus, and on each side of the entrance two altar-pieces, one representing the martyrdom of St. Catharine and the other that of St. Barbara; these are remarkable as works of art as well as for their antiquity.

At the further end of the hall is an altar, beautifully and elaborately carved in wood, the work of one of the lay-brothers; the altar-piece which is a Madonna of Corregio's is an exceedingly fine specimen of that master.

The apartments of the Religious are in the two wings of the Monastery which are connected with the eastern pavilion; they consist of the cells of the monks, the hall where prayers are said, the refectory and the recreation rooms.

Connected with these apartments is the seminary and rooms for the brothers and for novices who have a library of their own and a garden set apart for their special use. The Aspirants newly received into the order, are subjected to a severe novitiate of a year's duration under the superintendance of a Novice-master, when they take the simple vows and receive a new name. After three years further probation they take the solemn vows and are professed.

The College. The north pavilion with its adjoining wings is appropriated to the College which contains three halls for study, instruction being given in a great number of class and music rooms. A Chapel with beautiful frescos, and an altar-piece by Deschwanden is appropriated to the devotions of the boys and a sermon is preached to them there on Sundays and festivals.

Space has been found in this portion of the building for a school library, an infirmary and a small theatre.

The Library. This is in the north wing and is, next to the Church, the most important portion of the Monastery. A description of its contents will be given in a later chapter.

The Presbytery. The wing between the east pavilion and the Church has been set apart as a Presbytery for the use of the parishioners of Einsiedeln who are placed under the spiritual care of one of the Fathers, assisted by several Vicars chosen from among the ranks of the Monks.

The parish comprises not only the village proper of Einsiedeln, but also six out-lying hamlets.

The number of souls, according to the census taken in December 1880 amounts to 8403. As no parish Church now exists, the services are performed in one of the Chapels of the Monastery Church and in the Chapel attached to the neighbouring school.

The buildings adjoining the Monastery and comprised within its walls are devoted to the labourers and artizans connected with the Monastery; the space thus occupied is open to the public, access to it being obtained by means of a portal ornamented with a beautiful wrought iron grating situated at the extremity of the right wing of the principal facade. The corresponding portal at the extremity of the left wing gives access to the College. The buildings comprise dwellings

for the bailiff and for field-labourers, also a buttery,
a wash-house, and cow-houses, work-shops for car-
penters, wheelwrights etc. and an immense range
of stables. In the centre of the space encircled by
these constructions rises the tall chimney belonging
to the apparatus for heating the Monastery by
steam. The adjacent courts and gardens are surrounded by a wall of hewn stone which extends
from north to south along a space of 284 yards
and from east to west of 281 yards.

The interior of the Church.

CHAPTER IV.

The Church.

"THE Church of Einsiedeln", says a distinguished French traveller, "is the finest edifice which I have seen in Switzerland. Its situation in a solitary alpine valley and in the midst of lower buildings of simple construction, over which it towers, adds to the impression produced by the noble and harmonious style of its architecture while it affords a touching symbol of the protection which Religion ever extends to the poor and weak who fly to it for refuge."

The Church which stands in the centre of the Monastery has on either side of its principal entrance, a lofty and beautiful tower containing thirteen bells which, on occasion of great festivals, send forth their melodious peals, awaking the echoes of the mountains and filling the air with enchanting sounds.

The first object which strikes the eye on entering

is the small black marble building which rises in
the midst among the frescos and paintings like a
tomb in a garden of flowers. It is the Holy Chapel.
Advancing along the majestic nave the next
object which attracts special attention is a colos-

sal corona suspended from the central dome,
given by the Emperor Napoleon in 1865 in
memory of the pilgrimage made by his Mother
Queen Hortense to Our Lady of the Hermits.
This magnificent corona is of copper gilt, and
measures 4 yards in diameter by 6 yards and

a half in height. On a band which encircles it,
is inscribed in brilliant enamel the following words:
„I desire to place myself and my children under
the protection of the Blessed Virgin." These
words are taken from a letter written by Queen
Hortense to the Abbot of the Monastery. In
the interior of the corona is an imperial crown
with the inscription: „Given by Napoleon III,
Emperor of the French, 1865."

The Church is 125 yards long by 47 broad.
The nave is divided into three aisles, the central
one being 13 yards and a half wide. Eight
colossal columns support the vaulted roof, which
is decorated with frescos and golden arabesques.
All round the Church runs a Triforium con-
necting it with the Monastery and with the choir
occupied by the Monks. At 20 yards from the
great entrance the division into nave and aisles
ceases, and on either side of the space two isolated
pillars support a triumphal arch rising above the
Holy Chapel. To the right and left of the nave,
in the side arches, are fourteen Chapels, all of them
separated from the body of the Church by screens
of wrought iron, graceful and varied in design and
beautiful in execution. The altars are, generally
speaking, in the Italian style, the two largest being
of Einsiedeln marble; all of them are decorated
with reliquaries, statues, and paintings.

The first altar to the left is the altar of the
Rosary. It is of marble and in the modern Roman
style which although not in accordance with the
purest taste, is grandiose and impressive. On the
frontal of the altar, and at the base of the can-
delabra are small bas-reliefs in copper gilt representing the scenes of the Passion; these being the
only Stations of the Cross which the Church possesses. Statues of St. Matthew and St. Luke
stand on side pillars, and the summit of the altar
is adorned with a statue of the Archangel Raphael.
The picture over the altar represents the Blessed
Virgin giving the Rosary to St. Dominic, who is
kneeling at her feet, while in the background is
depicted the battle of Lepanto. This picture was
painted by Kraus, seven of whose productions are
to be seen at Einsiedeln. Death prevented him
from bringing his last work to a conclusion and
it was accordingly finished in 1752 by Weiss, a
native of Einsiedeln who had studied at Rome.

Near the altar stands a font for the parishioners of Einsiedeln. Since the removal of the
Parish Church the altar of the Rosary has been
appropriated to the use of the parish.

The fresco on the vault represents the dream
of the Patriarch Jacob. It is the work of Keller
of Pfrundten, who also executed the greater part
of the frescos in the Church.

The second altar to the left is dedicated to
St. Joseph. This altar is much smaller than the
preceding one, but it is equally harmonious in its
style. The body of the holy martyr Dionysius
rests in a sarcophagus above the altar and takes
the place generally occupied by a picture. The
statue of St. Joseph, as well as the allegorical figures
adorning this and other altars, are by Francis
Carloni of Lugano. They are remarkably graceful and refined in style, the heads of the Cherubim and the figures symbolising Innocence and
Truth being especially charming.

Innumerable marriages are celebrated throughout the year at the altar of St. Joseph, especially
between persons belonging to Einsiedeln and the
surrounding districts.

The third altar to the left is that of St. Meinrad,
and the two side altars are dedicated to St. Conrad
and St. Henry.

The small altar dedicated to the Holy Bishop
of Constance is adorned by one of the most beautiful master-pieces of Deschwanden; it consists
of a lifesize portrait of the Saint.

The large marble altar of St. Meinrad has
above it a picture representing St. Meinrad in the
desert, seeing in a vision the Blessed Virgin and
the Holy Child. In the back ground the murderers of the Saint are taking flight.

The fresco on the roof is a repetition of the picture over the altar and on one side is a smaller one representing God commanding Noah to build the Ark and bearing this inscription, „Fac tibi arcam et fœdus ponam tecum!" words which serve to remind the beholder that St. Meinrad in founding Einsiedeln was providing for many an ark of safety. Another fresco represents St. Meinrad in glory surrounded by angels. The altar is decorated with many excellent statues by Carloni, of the two largest one represents St. Wolfgang, Bishop of Ratisbon, and the other St. Eberhard, the first Abbot of Einsiedeln. Beneath the altar rest the remains of the holy martyr Vitalis.

Corresponding with the altar dedicated to St. Conrad is one to the right dedicated to the holy Emperor Henry, and over it is a picture of the Saint.

St. Wolfgang was St. Henry's patron. It was this pious Emperor who, when he was praying in the Church of St. Maria Maggiore at Rome, on the first night of his arrival there, saw „the sovereign and eternal Priest Christ-Jesus enter to say Mass. St. Lawrence and St. Vincent assisted as Deacon and Subdeacon, Saints innumerable filled the Church, and angels sang in the Choir. After the gospel an angel was sent by Our Lady to give him the book to bless. Tou-

ching Henry lightly on the thigh, as the angel did
to Jacob, he said: ‚Accept this sign of God's
love for your chastity and justice', and from that
time the Emperor always halted". St. Henry died
in the year 1022.

The fourth altar is dedicated to St. Maurice.
It is in the same style as that of St. Joseph and
may be appropriately termed the altar dedicated
to Christian Heroes. The three beautiful statues,
which are placed on it are by Carloni The
statue of St. Maurice, the patron of the Church at
Einsiedeln, with banner and lance in hand, stands
over the altar, whilst St Michael the Archangel,
is placed on the left and St. George on the right.
Beneath the altar lies the body of the holy martyr
Placidus. The fresco on the roof represents the
great benefactress of Einsiedeln, the holy empress
Adelheid, and another large fresco shows us St.
Maurice in glory, whilst St. Adelrich, a guardian of
the Monastery, holding a key in one hand leads
with the other his mother Regulina, the Duchess of
Germany. Behind them stand the Abbot Gregory,
St. Sigismund, his pupil, St. Placid, St. Wolfgang
and St. Thietland, the second Abbot of the Monas-
tery, with a book in his hand.

The fifth altar is dedicated to the Holy Cross.
It stands near the entrance to the Choir and
instead of a picture has over it a large bas-relief

representing the Saviour dying on the Cross, whilst above is a head of Our Blessed Lord. The statues of the Blessed Virgin and St. John, placed on either side of the altar, are remarkable for their expression of profound and dignified sorrow; they are considered to form the master-pieces, of Carloni whose work the bas-relief also is.

The relics venerated at this altar are those of one of the martyred soldiers of the Theban legion.

Passing in front of the Choir we come first to the Altar of the Mount of Olives.

This altar corresponds with that of the Holy Cross which has just been described. The bas-relief represents Our Lord praying on the Mount of Olives, above it is the head of the „Ecce homo". On either side are two beautiful life-size figures; one of St. John the Baptist, the other of Moses. There is also a group of angels weeping over the instruments of the Passion. In a reliquary the skull of the holy martyr Balbina is preserved.

The fresco represents, in common with that on the other side of the Choir, the Patrons of the Monastery. St. Gerold, with his two sons Kuno and Ulrich, look down from their seats in glory upon the Hermitage which they inhabited during their pilgrimage on earth. St. Sigismund, the King of Burgundy, is also there, and St. Scholastica with the dove, under the form of which her brother

saw her soul ascend to heaven. There, too, is the
Abbot Frederick who was thrown into prison by
certain wicked Monks, and near him is St. Gregory,
the third Abbot of the Monastery, who is being led
by an angel into the desert, and lastly St. Benno,
St. Meinrad's successor, who may be recognised
by his episcopal vestments and the knife with
which the burghers of Metz thrust out his eyes.

The seventh altar is dedicated to St. Sigismund.
Of this holy King of Burgundy the Monastery
has from the earliest times possessed some precious relics. His altar is immediately opposite that
of St. Maurice, and may be designated as the altar
of Christian Monarchs, seeing that it is adorned
with statues of three Royal Saints. Above the
Altar is the statue of St. Sigismund himself, at
his side is St. Ursula with a crown on her head,
whilst in her hand she holds the arrows with which
her arms and breast were pierced. On the other
side of the King is the holy Adelheid, the wife
of the Emperor Otho the Great. On the altar rest
the remains of the Roman martyr Candida. The
fresco on the roof represents the holy Emperor
Henry II, who, it may be stated, was a great
Benefactor to the Monastery.

The eighth altar is dedicated to St. Benedict,
and the two side-altars to the Sacred Heart of
Jesus and the Sacred Heart of Mary.

In this Chapel is represented the order under whose banner the monks of Einsiedeln live and labour. The subject of the beautiful altar-piece is the death of St. Benedict and is the work of the brother of Carloni. Here again, as in the altar-piece of St. Meinrad's Chapel, the contrast between heaven and earth is portrayed, and the way pointed out by which Our Saviour passed to His Father and by which also St. Benedict ascends to Paradise.

On either side of the altar stand two exceedingly striking statues, one of them representing Gregory the Great, who wrote the life of the Founder of the order, the other Pope Zacharias, who gave his sanction to the rule of St. Benedict. Three other statues adorn the altar and are allegorical representations of the rule of St. Benedict and of the vows required from his disciples. The figure on the right hand pillar symbolises Chastity, that on the left, Obedience, while the sacred words of Poverty and Fidelity are inscribed on small scrolls in the hands of Cherubim; lastly on the summit of the altar the female figure bearing a torch is the Rule personified, the book she holds in her hand being open at the page inscribed *Ausculta* etc.

It is needless to say that it is to the chisel of Carloni these graceful and striking statues are due.

The fresco shows us God the Father giving to Abraham the promise of an innumerable pos- terity, as contained in the words „Faciam te in gentem magnam, erisque benedictus" being a play upon the word *benedictus*, which signifies Blessed. St. Benedict is moreover represented in glory surrounded by angels, one of whom holds a branch from which thorns and roses spring and which bears allusion to St. Benedict hav- ing conquered the impure thoughts that were besieging him by throwing himself naked into a thorn-bush on which roses immediately blossomed.

The corpse of the Roman martyr Gregory rests below the altar which was erected in 1739 by Franzlin of Bregenz, who had formerly been a Novice in the Convent. At the side-altars de- dicated to the Sacred Heart of Jesus and the Sacred Heart of Mary mass is said uninterrup- tedly for several hours every morning, and de- vout persons are never wanting to assist at it.

The ninth altar is consecrated to St. Anne. It corresponds to the small altar of St. Joseph. Above the altar is placed the statue of St. Anne teaching her holy daughter to read. To the left and right are statues of Hope and Love by Carloni. The reliquary contains the body of the holy martyr Charitosa with the sword symbolising, as in the case of other martyrs whose relics are preserved in the

Church, the manner of her martyrdom, such being also the system adopted in the Catacombs of Rome.

The tenth altar is that of the Confraternity of Our Lady of the Hermits.

This altar is in the modern Italian style and is profusely decorated with marbles, gilding etc. Its construction cost 18,000 Italian lire. The picture on the anti-pendium represents the Divine Dedication, and the beautiful altar-piece is the first work produced by the artist Kraus after his return from France. He appears to have taken special pains with the composition which represents Our Lady of the Hermits and the Patroness of Christians. Her beautiful and graceful form floats on the air, and her blue mantle envelopes the Holy Chapel on which a miraculous light streams down from heaven. Groups of angels separate the upper portion of the picture from the lower, on which all descriptions of human suffering are depicted This picture, as well as the others which decorate the Chapel, was skilfully restored in the year 1844. The statues on either side of the altar, placed upon pillars, represent St. John and St. Mark whilst between them is St. Michael holding the sceptre of the heavenly choir. The fresco represents Our Saviour with Zaccheus.

The Choir.

The lower choir is in a different style of architecture from that of the nave, which was constructed at a later period and therefore forms a striking contrast to it. Allegorical frescos and beautiful golden arabesques are abundantly employed
and the whole of the decoration makes a deep
impression on the pilgrim, awaking emotions
which the splendours of a dwelling dedicated to
the Majesty of the Most High God are ever
calculated to excite.

Outside the Choir and facing the nave are
two marble monuments which may be regarded
as the farewell of Carloni to his admirers, seeing
that they were the last works which proceeded from
his chisel. In the pavement immediately below
the monument to the right is a stone, which on being
raised gives entrance to the burial-vaults of the
monks. The Choir is separated from the nave
by a very beautiful and artistic iron screen of which
kind of work numerous and exquisite specimens
are to be found in the Church. The coat of
arms introduced in the iron-work proves that this
screen dates from the time of the earlier Church and
was placed there by the Abbot Augustus Reding
as the lilies of his crest occur continually in it.

The great frescos which decorate the roof or
the Choir may be divided into different portions,
the whole forming a complete representation of
the Sacrifice of the New Testament.

·The large frescos above the centre of the
Choir represent the Lamb of God who, dying
on the Cross, sheds His Blood for the salvation
of the world. Before the Lamb kneel the four
and twenty elders of the Apocalypse, whilst in the
background the jewish high priest, overwhelmed
with fear, takes flight.

In another fresco, the Son of God appears
before the Almighty Father and offers Himself a
Sacrifice for man. The Archangel Gabriel is about
hastily to depart to announce the mystery to Mary,
whilst on the other side angels are depicted bearing
in their hands the instruments of the Passion. In
the foreground the kings and peoples of the Old
Testament are seen standing or kneeling, Abraham
with his son Isaac and king David being the most
conspicuous figures.

These immense frescos are surrounded by
five smaller, the subjects of which are taken
from the Old Testament, and are also connected
with the idea of the great Sacrifice of Jesus. They
are the work of the artist Rüep of Augsburg and of
Kraus, whose name has been already mentioned,
and who also painted the magnificent picture re-

Deschwanden's Assumption over the High-Altar.

presenting the dying Christ, which is placed in the upper Choir set apart for the monks. Kraus spent part of his life at Einsiedeln and died while painting the head of the Blessed Virgin in the Rosary Chapel.

Two bas-reliefs in the centre of the Choir represent the Sacrifice of Melchisedech and that offered by Aaron. The accompanying decorations also carry out the same idea as that symbolised by the frescos and bas-reliefs.

The high-altar, which is 16 yards distant from the beautiful and exquisitely wrought iron screen, separating the Choir from the nave, was executed by Pozzi of Milan in marble, from a drawing of Torricelli's and cost 27,000 lire. It was begun in the year 1749 and finished in 1751.

Set in the centre of it is a bas-relief in bronze, also by Pozzi, representing the last supper.

Thus, as in the frescos on the roof is given a representation of the heavenly conception of the Sacrifice of Jesus, so on the altar below is shown forth how the Sacrifice is continually solemnized and repeated on earth, to the truth of which the animals typifying the Evangelists and the angels with grapes and ears of corn, placed at the corners of the altar, also bear witness. Above the altar is Our Blessed Lord on the Cross, a work of rare merit, as is also the representation of the Resurrection on the door of the Tabernacle.

On the side walls are four bas-reliefs representing events in the life of the Blessed Virgin who had so large a share in the work of redemption, and crowning all there rises in the background the picture of the Assumption of Our Lady, painted in oil on the wall. This picture, as well as the whole of the frescos in the choir, was retouched and greatly altered in the summer of 1857—1858 by Deschwanden. The divinely inspired pencil of the Master has given quite a new character to it. The artist, who, to the great grief of all who knew him and his works, died on the 25th February 1881, held Einsiedeln in especial reverence and often resorted thither as a pilgrim to offer up his prayers to Our Lady. Nowhere are to be found such numerous and beautiful productions of his pencil as at Einsiedeln. Another great artist of his time was Franz Kraus who was born at Augsburg 1706, and spent four years at Einsiedeln 1745—1749 during which years he executed the greater portion of the frescos in the choir as well as several of the altar-pieces. In 1752 he planned and executed all the decorations of the lower choir and had also undertaken the construction of the upper choir when he died in 1755. His remains rest

in the cemetery at Einsiedeln. — In a gallery near
the picture of the Assumption are four colossal
statues, of which one of them, representing Innocence, was thrown down in the time of the
French Revolution, but a new one was, at a later
period placed there.

The upper Choir.

The wall on which the picture of the Assumption is painted separates the lower from the upper
Choir; the latter being set apart for the monks.
Divided as it is by the wall from the Church it
forms, so to speak, an independent building, but
on both sides of the picture a good view is
obtained into the nave from between six pillars
of black marble.

On the altar is a beautiful Tabernacle of carved
wood, cased in silver, and in it are preserved several precious relics of St. Benedict which were
presented to the Monastery on the 14th of August
1857 by the Bishop of Orleans. The paintings
with which the whole of the Choir is decorated
are by the artist Torricelli. In his works he
shows more of skill than of genius, nevertheless
they give evidence of great power and thereby
raise him to a high position among fresco painters.
The subjects of these frescos are either connected

with choral song or with those which characterise
the frescos of the lower choir.

In the middle of the choir are two immense
lecturns on which are placed two great parchment
choir-books, in the composition of which F^r John
Häfele was engaged, during the 17th century, for
the space of twenty years. They are decorated
with very beautiful illuminations and are still used
in the Choir.

An excellent double organ daily accompanies
the choral offices, but it is not favourably placed,
buried as it is in the wall; it suffered greatly
during the French Revolution and has since that
period been frequently restored.

It may here be remarked that there are two
new organs in the gallery of the Church, one
near the altar of St. Benedict, the other near that
of St. Meinrad, of which the larger was built by
Kiene of Kislegg.

The frescos on the cupolas in the nave.

These decorations are in quite a different style
of art from those of the Choir and are characteri-
zed by great brilliancy and freedom, as indeed is
the case with all the frescos painted by Cosmas
Asam, a Bavarian artist of the last century who
executed these works.   His youthful heads have

an indescribable charm whilst the grandeur and boldness of his designs are very appropriate to the vast dimensions of the Church.

On the first of the three great cupolas of the nave is depicted the Nativity. It was a difficult task to fill so large a space with one sole subject, but the artist has been wonderfully successful in his attempt. The figure of the Eternal Father contemplating from the upper portion of the cupola the magnificent representation of the Nativity beneath Him was painted, it is said, by the artist during the mid-day repast of the community. The monks on entering the Church after their meal saw the sky opened and the Glory of Heaven revealed to their astonished eyes.

The second cupola represents the Last Supper. This fresco is full of life and movement. The principal groups are especially beautiful, and as admirable in conception as they are skilful in execution. If there is any fault to be found with the work, it lies in its very beauty, that is to say, in the wealth of accessories which it displays.

The third cupola which rises above the Holy Chapel, is larger than the two others and is separated into four parts which, meeting together, repose upon the two pillars on either side of the Holy Chapel. Asam to whom was committed the decoration of this cupola, has depicted upon it in glowing colours the history of the Divine Dedication. In the centre the Saviour, surrounded by angels bearing the sacerdotal vestments, descends from heaven, whilst in the space on one side of Him, preparations are being made for the solemn ceremonial and on the other side another series of preparations are going on. Opposite the Christ and above the portion occupied by kneeling pilgrims, the Blessed Virgin, the Queen of Heaven, for whom the Divine Consecration of the Chapel was celebrated, bears in her hand the sceptre of her kingdom; myriads of angels surround her while she looks down radiantly upon her people.

In the gallery over the great doors of the Church are represented the Faithful, amongst whom is St. Conrad, hastening to the celebration of the consecration of the Sanctuary. But they all suddenly halt upon hearing a voice descending from heaven and exclaiming „Cease brother, cease, the Chapel is divinely consecrated". In the background is represented the dedication of the Temple of Solomon; a beautiful type of the consecration of the Holy Chapel.

The Penitentiary.

In addition to the great Church there is on the left of the Choir a Chapel dedicated to

St. Mary Magdalen, otherwise styled the Penitentiary, because it is used for the Sacrament of Penance. It was built by the Abbot Augustine II, about the year 1680, over a cemetery. At a former period this Chapel was remarkable for the wealth of its decorations, the frescos adorning the roof being especially held in high esteem. But since then they have been superseded by a series of paintings which form a gallery of representations of penance taken from the Scriptures and from the lives of the Saints. The architecture of the Chapel is rather heavy in style, the roof is supported by six marble pillars and the choir is entirely separated from the nave; its cupola is very elevated and decorated with appropriate frescos. The altar-piece represents a Magdalen painted· by Gaspard Sing of Munich and is undoubtedly the finest picture on canvas possessed by the community. On each side of the nave are placed nine and twenty confessionals, and there are days and weeks during the year when this chapel, which is capable of containing fifteen hundred people, is filled with pilgrims from morning to night, whilst numbers wait for hours outside the door till they can obtain entrance.

CHAPTER V.

The Holy Chapel.

WHEN St. Eberhard united together the Oratory and Cell of St. Meinrad and enclosed them within the great Church, the walls of the Holy Chapel were constructed of wood, but of the building as it existed in its original state, no account or illustration has come down to us; it may, however, be taken for granted that it was of very simple construction. Neither have we any description of the edifice of stone, which was erected at a later period; we can therefore only form a conjecture as to its primary appearance.

After the great fire of 1467, which has been described in a foregoing chapter, the Bishop of Constance directed that the Holy Chapel should be arched over,. and on the persons employed in the work stating. it to be their opinion that the walls had been built by very inefficient workmen he directed that they should be strengthened and furnished with pillars and pilasters of stone. He also employed a certain „Master Schleerbach" of Bâle to paint the ceiling over it at his own cost. About the year 1617 the pillars erected by the Bishop of Constance were taken down and the whole of the Chapel faced with marble under the superintendence of Marcus Sitticus, Archbishop of Salzburg. In 1730 the Prince Abbot Thomas removed the ceiling, and surrounded the top of the walls with a marble balustrade. At the last restoration of the Holy Chapel, which was effected after the French Revolution, as much as possible of its former proportions and characteristics were retained, and the exterior is at present, as it was at an earlier date, a structure of black marble, with the exception of the capitals of the pillars and of the bas-reliefs which are of white marble. It measures 8 yards and a half in length by 6 yards in breadth and is 5 yards and a half high. To the front is a great portal, 2 yards broad by 4 yards and a half high, made of wrought iron of very beautiful design; on either sidewall are also doors of wrought iron richly ornamented and opening into the Chapel. The bas-reliefs of the Nativity of the Blessed Virgin and of the Annunciation were formerly placed beside the one representing the death of Our Blessed Lady, but they now occupy a position where they can be better seen.

The Holy Chapel.

The statues which decorate the front-angles of
the balustrade represent St. Meinrad, St. Adelrich,
St. Benno and St. Conrad, the statue of the
Blessed Virgin Immaculate occupying a position
between the two last; at her feet on the exterior
wall of the Chapel is an inscription in latin, stating
that Marcus Sitticus, Archbishop of Salzburg, faced
the wooden walls of the Chapel with marble.
In the interior, the walls of the upper portion
are covered with stucco up to the vault which
rises in the form of a cupola. The lower portion
of the Chapel is decorated with Carrara and
other marbles. Above the altar stands St. Meinrad's statue of the Blessed Virgin. It is of wood
and very massive; the drapery, which is uncom-
monly noble and beautiful in its simple folds
was, at an earlier period, ornamented in colours
and gold. The Child, who is on the left arm
of His Mother, holds in His hand a little bird
which is pecking it. The faces and hands of
both figures are black, as is the case with the
majority of ancient representations of the Blessed Virgin venerated by pilgrims. Whether the
colour is symbolical, or only the effect of smoke
is a question not yet decided. In any case the
blackness is not the natural colour of the wood.
As a work of art the statue has always been
a problem difficult of solution. Distinguished

The altar of the Holy Chapel.

artists and antiquarians consider it to be a remarkable specimen of early Christian art and in
its treatment and conception find a proof that
it belongs to a period much earlier in date than
that of the later middle ages, although it shows
no signs of the stiffness, heaviness, and want of
correctness which distinguish the generality of
old German statues. There is no evidence, however, that its origin is to be sought for in the
East, although an old tradition declares it to have
been brought from thence by the Crusaders, for
there is no indication of Byzantine character in
any portion of the statue and least of all in the
face. It is most probable that it belongs to the
period of St. Meinrad and is a work of the
ninth century.

The statue is clothed in garments made of
cloth of gold, and on the heads of Mother and
Child are placed golden crowns set with precious
stones. Five silver lamps, the gifts of royal and
aristocratic personages, used to burn night and
day before it, and in front of the altar were
formerly sixteen great tapers, which were kept
constantly burning at the expense of the Catholic
Cantons who loved to see typified in the perpetual
flame, their own constancy and faith. These
tapers weighed from 20 to 30 kilogrammes each
and their brilliant light formed a glowing back-

ground to the statue. But the golden decorations are gone, the silver lamps have disappeared and given place to copper and the silver bas-reliefs representing the Divine Dedication, which formerly adorned the altar, are no longer to be seen. The flaming tapers were extinguished in the political tempests, which desolated Switzerland, but the most ancient ornament of the Chapel and the one which evil men and conquerors have over and over again attempted to destroy, still remains intact, for the miraculous statue, after a short exile from the Holy Chapel during the period of the French Revolution, returned once more to its former home where it still continues, year by year, to receive the homage of above a hundred thousand pilgrims. The altar of the Holy Chapel, made of Carrara marble, is the work of the artist Argentini of Vieggiu; on its frontal is a bas-relief in brass of the Divine Dedication designed by J. J. Wikart of Einsiedeln and executed by Manfredini of Milan. It was presented to the Chapel by Charles Albert, King of Sardinia. On either side of the altar are reliefs in gilt bronze, one representing the statue of the Blessed Virgin being conveyed to the hermitage of St. Meinrad, and the other the death of the Saint. On the altar is a reliquary containing the head of the Servant of God.

ABBOT BASIL

BORN THE 28TH DEC. 1821. PROFESSED THE 24TH SEPT. 1843.
ELECTED ABBOT THE 18TH JAN. 1878.

CHAPTER VI.

The Benedictine Fathers of Einsiedeln.

EVER since the time that the Convent of
Einsiedeln developed itself from its humble origin
in St. Meinrad's cell into a vast Benedictine
Monastery, its influence has made itself perceptible
far and wide, as well as in its more immediate
surroundings, and this not only in matters solely
concerning the spiritual life, but also in those
associated with secular culture. In its early days
whoever showed a desire to lead an industrious
and holy life was sure of receiving encouragement
and · aid from the Religious, whilst the devout
crowds who in ever-increasing numbers went year
after year on pilgrimage to the Holy Chapel and
who assisted at the solemn and beautiful functions, celebrated in·the Church, received a most
wholesome influence and spread it over a wide
extent of country.

The esteem in which the Monks of Einsiedeln

were held soon reached an extraordinary, height
and from every side the flower of the nobility
and the most enlightened men of the ages of
Faith pressed for admittance into the ranks of
the Monks. On the other hand the Fathers were
frequently raised to Episcopal Sees or elected
Abbots over newly established Foundations.

To the universal respect and reverence in
which the Benedictine Fathers at Einsiedeln have
always been held must also be ascribed the valuable
gifts with which Emperors and Princes have, at
different periods, enriched the Monastery. Amongst
these may be named the Island of Ufnau on the
Lake of Zurich, presented by the Emperor Otho I
to the Convent, with all the rights thereto appertaining. Similar gifts were made to the Fathers by other Emperors and in particular by
Henry II, surnamed „the pious". Otho and Henry
may indeed be considered as the greatest of the
many Benefactors of the Monastery, the year book
of which mentions them with exceeding gratitude
and their statues still adorn the great stone balustrade in front of the Church.

Abbot Gregory, in whom the English Church
has a special interest on account of his being a
descendant of Alfred the Great, was invested by
Otho III. with the dignity of a Prince of the
Empire, which investiture was renewed in favour

of Abbot Ulrich II. and his successors by King
Rudolph of Habsburg in the year 1274. Baron
Gerold, of Hohensax in Graubunden, both of
whose sons had become Monks at Einsiedeln,
gave to the Convent a forest (Wildniss) in the
Vorarlberg where he had lived for a long time
as a hermit. This forest bears a great resemblance to Einsiedeln and was named by the Monks
after St. Gerold, whose life, as has already been
mentioned, was written by Walter von Bonstetten.
Many costly reliquaries, holy vessels, and other
church-treasure were in like manner presented to
the Monastery, and although in the stormy times
of war, during the so-called Reformation, and
the French Revolution, a great many of these
gifts were lost, or were sacrificed to meet pressing
necessities, the grateful remembrance of the donors
still dwells in the hearts of the Monks of Einsiedeln.

Severe indeed were the storms which at different times swept over the Monastery, especially
during the period when the Catholic Church in
Switzerland was torn by internal dissensions.

In the year 1526, after the death of Prince
Abbot Conrad III., the Convent was left almost
destitute of monks, and the greater part of its
possessions was seized by the followers of Zwingle
whilst the small remainder was laden with debts.
At last, after repeated appeals and representations

addressed by the inhabitants of the Canton of Schwytz to the government, Ludwig Blarer, one of the most distinguished of the Monks of the old Benedictine Abbey of St. Gall, was summoned to Einsiedeln. With the utmost diligence and zeal he at once set himself to educate young men to enter the order and to bring back again the possessions which had been alienated from the Monastery. In this good work he was greatly assisted by the Catholic Cantons and the Emperor of Austria. Up to that time the Monastery seems only to have been open to the highest members of the nobility and therefore the number of its Religious was relatively small, but under its reorganisation by Ludwig Blarer all were received without distinction of rank who, in addition to possessing a vocation for the religious life, showed the necessary qualifications for filling the various offices in the community. The labours undertaken by the Monks are of a varied description but the Convent of the holy St. Meinrad is specially a school for wisdom and virtue. Great is the number of the Fathers who have distinguished themselves by their holiness, their science and their sagacity in the administration of temporal affairs. Many have been inscribed by the Church in her Calendar of Saints. Others, called to preside over the Episcopal sees of Metz, Ratis-

bon, Constance, Chur and Como, have ruled
their dioceses with wisdom and zeal: others again
have been called upon to occupy the Chair of
Professors in the High Schools of Germany,
and have been elected members of scientific
associations.

Very great has also been the mumber of those
who, in the stillness and silence of their cells, have
benefitted their fellow men by the composition
of learned works and spiritual treatises, others
again have been distinguished by a holy zeal in
the winning of souls.

The rule of the Monastery has always been that
of St. Benedict, modified, under the approbation
of the Sovereign Pontiff, by special constitutions.

The days of the Benedictines at Einsiedeln
are devoted to Prayer, to the Confessional, to
Teaching, to Study, and to the fine arts.

1stly Prayer. The offices in the Choir begin
at the same hour as the first Mass in the Holy
Chapel, i. e. at four o'clock in the morning. Ma-
tins last one hour and are terminated by the Te
Deum and Lauds, accompanied on Feast-days
by the organ. The Masses in the Holy Chapel
and at all the numerous altars in the Church
follow one after another without interruption for
several hours, the Mass at six o clock being
reserved for special Foundations. At seven o'clock

Prime and Tierce are said and are immediately
followed by the Conventual High Mass, celebrated
at the High altar; it is sung to the accompaniment of either a full orchestra, or else of a simple
choir of voices with an organ. The Fathers are
admirably aided in this respect by the pupils
belonging to the College of the Monastery, who
assist at all the great offices. After High Mass
Sext and None are said. On Sundays and festivals
a sermon is preached at eight o' clock and whilst
it lasts no masses or offices go on. At three
o' clock every day vespers are chanted, after
which the Religious, who have taken part in the
office, preceded by some of their pupils, descend
into the Church and walk in procession down
one of the aisles with slow step and grave demeanour until, arrived at the Holy Chapel, they
kneel upon the marble pavement and sing the
Salve Regina. When it is well executed, and
when the listener has chosen his position at some
distance from the Chapel this chant, which is a
composition of the eleventh century, is very
solemn and impressive, adapted as it is to one
of the most beautiful odes of the Catholic Church.
Compline, which is chanted at seven o' clock,
concludes the services of the day.

2dly The Confessional. The cares and duties
appertaining to this priestly office absorb a large

portion of the time of the Fathers and are as fatiguing as they are important. The number of Confessors varies according to the time of year, the greatest demand being from Easter to the end of October. Sundays and festivals are naturally the days when most pilgrims resort to the Church; on each of such occasions thousands assemble there, the majority having been to confession on the vigil of the Feast. The average number of confessions is reckoned at 154,000 yearly and to meet such an immense demand requires the combined force of all the available Priests.

3dly Teaching and Study. The College of Einsiedeln can look back on many a past century. St. Meinrad, being a distinguished teacher of youth, may be regarded as its founder. After him the first name distinguished in history is that of St. Wolfgang, who died Bishop of Ratisbon in 994. Another remarkable name is that of Rudolf von Radegg, the poet, who taught in the College in the fourteenth century. For nearly two hundred years the Convent had a branch-school at Bellinzona in Canton Tessin, which was dissolved by the government in 1852 just when it had attained its most flourishing state and numbered 90 scholars. This event led to the enlarging of the College at Einsiedeln

which, up to that period, had not had more than
forty pupils at one time. The new Abbot, Heinrich
Schmid, as soon as he had been elected, made it
his first care to provide accommodation for the
scholars who had been sent from Bellinzona and
at the same time he enlarged the scope of their
studies. New life was infused into the College.
Young and able men were sent to foreign lands
to be trained as Professors, a school-library
was established, and means for study provided
so that, in a very short space of time, the school
was in a position to take its stand among the
first Catholic Schools in Switzerland. A further
step in advance has been taken under the rule
of the present Abbot Basil who was formerly
one of the most distinguished Professors in the
College. In the year 1883, the number of pupils
had risen to about 300.

The course of instruction is the same for
boarders and day pupils and a term of eight
years is divided between a Gymnasium and a
Lyceum. The Gymnasium comprises courses of
study in Latin, Greek, German and Religion,
lasting for six years, the lessons in these various
branches being given by the same Professor,
whilst instruction in Mathematics, History and
Physics is given by different Professors. The
Lyceum habitually numbers about 40 pupils under

six Professors, who, in the first yearly course, teach philosophy in all its essential branches, the second year being devoted to the study of Astronomy, Chemistry &c. Lessons are also given in modern languages, French, Italian, English, and in Music, Singing and Drawing.

Such of the Fathers who are not otherwise engaged, work in their cells. Some give themselves up to the study of the Scriptures and Theology; others occupy themselves with various periods of Ecclesiastical History, others again penetrate into the mysteries of science. Among these last may be numbered the inventor of an ingenious machine connected with the electric telegraph. Others devote themselves to painting, others to the composition of music and others again to poetry.

For the rest, the distinguished labours of the Religious at Einsiedeln have always been recognised by learned and scientific societies. For instance, in 1865, when the University of Vienna celebrated the five hundredth anniversary of its foundation, it remembered the Convent of Einsiedeln, its senior by five hundred years and conferred the degree of D. D. on F[r] Brandes, on account of his authorship of several scientific books and of his historical researches in connection with the Order of St. Benedict. F[r] Gall Morel, who

died in 1872, is known as a distinguished poet
far and wide; as a connoisseur of Art and a
Musician. He ranks also amongst the most
distinguished Theologians, Philologists and Libra-
rians of the Convent. A memoir of him entitled
„The life of a Monk in the 19th century" has been
published by Fr Benno Kühne; it is impossible
to imagine a more interesting work, showing as
it does in a most vivid and striking manner how
many-sided a man Fr Gall Morel was, how full
of interest was his career, and how beneficial
and elevating was the influence which this admirable Monk exerted over all who came in
contact with him; above all how lasting and excellent was the effect produced by his teaching
on the hearts and minds of his pupils, many of
whom confess that, humanly speaking, they owe
all the good that is in them and the whole of
their success in life to the lessons given them
and the example set them by their beloved and
lamented Professor.

In order to aid them in their studies the Monks
possess a Library of over 30,000 volumes, among
which are to be found several remarkable works,
comprising a great many Bibles in different languages and about 900 black-letter editions. Very
important and curious is also the collection of
manuscripts, among which one is to be found

more than a thousand years old. The most
remarkable of these manuscripts is a so-called
Regionator Einsidlensis, or collection of latin
epigraphs written down on the spot by a pilgrim
of the 8th century. Very interesting also are certain books of prayer with the old musical notation,
amongst which may be mentioned a splendid
antiphonarium. The number of printed books is
continually receiving fresh additions through do-
nations, or by purchase. The same may be said
of the collection of minerals and other illustrations
of natural history which are daily made use of in
the interests of science and in the studies carried
on in the College. Another special merit distin-
guishes the Fathers at Einsiedeln for, amongst the
religious associations which have of late made
such strenuous efforts to withdraw Church music
from the beaten track it has hitherto followed,
the Benedictines have acquired a special title to
the gratitude of real artists. Faithful to the
traditions of their illustrious predecessors they
have always assigned to music its proper pro-
vince. Of old the Fathers held that one of the
most honorable of the offices they could be called
upon to fill was that of the Cantor who, was
it were, a living diapason imposing on the choir
the unity of his voice until, at a later period, the
organ was introduced. But neither organ nor

song forms the entire orchestre at Einsiedeln, wind and stringed instruments being also used by experienced and skilful musicians. ˌˌ·

Of the organs placed by the Abbot Augustin I. in the great Church, which, on the occasion of solemn festivals are made to discourse exquisite music, and to hold ravishing dialogues with each other, raising the soul of the listener to heaven, we have already spoken.

The musical archives of the Monastery are being continually enriched by the compositions of the Fathers. They can also boast a very valuable collection of musical works, amongst which may be mentioned those of our English composer Pearsall, whose portrait the Monks are proud to possess.

Fʳ Schubiger, ex-director of the musical department of Einsiedeln, has earned the gratitude of all true friends of art by a collection of thirty beautiful airs composed by him in honour of the Blessed Virgin. This little book which bears the title of „Roses of Mary" has reached its tenth edition in Germany and has also been published in France and Spain. Fʳ Schubiger has also recently published a work full of erudition, which throws great light on the question of liturgical song; it is entitled the „School of Song at St. Gall from the sixth to the twelfth century" and is enriched with fac-similes remarkable for their execution.

But the labours and good works of the Fathers do not end here. Though too numerous to mention in detail, reference may be made to a guild for working men and apprentices, which they have established in a portion of the Convent. Every evening, between six and ten, the members gather together, some of them to receive instruction from the Monks, others to listen to lectures, others to practise drawing, or to devote themselves to one or another branch of study likely to be useful to them in their daily life.

Nor must the Lay-brothers, who are already monks, though not Priests, be forgotten. To them is committed the care of the Church and the menial offices necessary in the Monastery, also the nursing of the sick and infirm.

Thirty-four of the Fathers are employed as Parish priests; these have the care of seven Parishes; others administer the estates belonging to the Monastery and superintend the stables, which are celebrated for a peculiar and beautiful breed of horses of which the community at present possesses over seventy. Other Fathers of Einsiedeln have gone out as Missionaries to North America where they have founded a Monastery of St. Meinrad in Spencer County Indiana.

A Procession in Einsiedeln.

CHAPTER VII.

The Pilgrimage.

It is to the Pilgrimage made to Our Lady of the Hermits that Einsiedeln owes its fame, and the inhabitants of the village, in a great measure, their livelihood.

The pilgrims come principally from the Catholic Cantons of Switzerland, and from the borders of France, Germany and Italy, and even from America, Asia and Africa. Amongst them are often to be found personages of the highest rank, both clerical and lay, as will be seen by the following extracts, taken from the lists of visitors which have been kept at the Monastery from the earliest times.

In the year

915. *Adalbert*, Bishop of Bâle, a relative of St. Benno.

955. The Emperor *Otho*, the Great, and *St. Adelheid*, his spouse.

900—972. *St. Ulrich, St. Wolfgang* and *St. Gerold.*

In the year

1100. *Ulrich,* Count of Kyburg, Bishop of Constance, who consecrated the altar of. St. John in the Church.

1141. *Theodewin,* Papal Nuncio to Germany, Cardinal-bishop of Porto.

1335. *St. Elizabeth,* daughter of Andrew III., King of Hungary.

1353. King *Charles IV.* with a great suite of Princes and Prelates.

1442. *Frederick III.,* Emperor of Rome.

1576. *St. Charles Borromeo,* Cardinal-Archbishop of Milan.

1589. *Octavius Pallavicini,* who received the Cardinal's hat, when he was on a pilgrimage to Einsiedeln.

1595 and onwards. The Princes and Princesses of Hohenzollern.

1622. *Louis XIII.,* King of France.

1683. F^r *Mabillon,* a learned Benedictine of the Convent of St. Maur.

1775. *St. Benedict Joseph Labre,* who made the pilgrimage several times. — *Goethe,* the German poet, who visited Einsiedeln a second time in 1797.

1793. The *Archbishop of Paris,* accompanied by many refugee Priests.

1813. *Ludwig I.,* King of Bavaria.

1814. The Archduke *Nicholas,* afterwards Emperor of Russia; also Archduke *Romanow* and the ex-Empress, *Louise,* Duchess of Parma.

1816. Queen *Hortense,* who made pilgrimages to Einsiedeln several times, between the years 1816 and 1823, being accompanied on some of these occasions by her son, *Louis Napoleon.*

1819. *Frederick William,* Crown Prince.of Prussia, afterwards King; also *Frederick,* Prince of Holland, and

In the year
> *Ludwig,* Crown Prince, and afterwards King of Bavaria.

1820. Prince *Charles Esterhazy.* — *Ignatius Naffali,* Archbishop of Tyre, Apostolical Nuncio in Switzerland, and afterwards Cardinal.

1826. *Frederick Charles Christian,* Prince of Denmark. Several members of the Chamber at Frankfurt.

1829. The Duke de *Rohan,* Card.-Archbishop of Besançon.

1831. *William,* King of Wurtemberg.

1835. *Ferdinand,* Duke of Orleans. — *Marie Isabella* of Bourbon, and the widowed Queen of Naples.

1838. Mgr. *Dupanloup,* Grandvicar of Paris, later Bishop of Orleans.

1840. Count *Neukomm,* the musical composer.

1842. Mgr. *Polding,* Benedictine Archbishop of Sydney in Australia.

1843. Mgr. *Purcell,* Bishop of Cincinnati, North-America. Fr *Lacordaire,* Dominican Monk.

1852. Professor *Döllinger* of Munich.

1854. Mgr. *Dupanloup,* Bishop of Orleans.

1857. Mgr. *Ullathorne,* Bishop of Birmingham. — Mgr. *Dupanloup.* — Mgr. de *Bonnechose,* Cardinal-Archbishop of Rouen.

1859. Mgr. *St. Palais,* Bishop of Vincennes, North-America. — *Louise Marie,* Duchess of Parma. — Prince *Henry,* Count of Bardi. — Princess *Margaret* of Bourbon. — *Henry,* Count of Chambord.

1860. Mgr. *Hartmann,* Bishop of Patna, East-India.

1861. YEAR OF THE GREAT JUBILEE. Numerous Archbishops and Bishops. — Prince *Chigi,* Apostolical Nuncio at Paris. — A great number of Abbots. — The Duchesses of Parma and Berri. — The Princesses

In the year

Sidonia and *Sophia* of Saxony. — *Margaret* and *Alice* of Bourbon. — Princess *Caroline* of Hohenzollern. — Princess *Galitzin.* — Princess of Windishgrätz. — The Archduke *Ferdinand* of Tuscany. — *Charles Ludwig* of Austria. — Prince *Adalbert* of Bavaria. — Prince *George* of Saxony. — Prince *Humbert* and Prince *Amadeus* of Savoy. — Baron of *Mayenfisch*, as representative of the King of Prussia, and about 2000 ecclesiastics from all parts of the world. *)

1862. The Archbishops and Bishops *Schwarzenberg* of Prague, *Furstenberg* of Olmütz, *Fessler* of Nyssa &c. *Louise,* Duchess of Parma. — *Amelia,* Princess of Fürstenberg. — Princess of Baden. — *Elise,* Princess of Fürstenberg. — The princely family of Hohenzollern-Sigmaringen.

1863. The Archbishops and Bishops *Falcinelli,* Nuncio at Vienna, *Johann* of Soissons, *Langalerie* of Belley, *Marilley* of Friburg. — *Augustus,* Prince of Saxe-Coburg-Gotha. — *Clementine* of Orleans, Princess of Saxe-Coburg, with Prince *Philip* and Princess *Amelia.* — *Clotilde* of Saxe-Coburg. — *Eleanor,* Princesse of Salm. — The Princesses *Francisca* and *Therese Lichtenstein.* — Duchess of Berri. — *Louis* of Orleans, Duke of Nemours. — *Margaret* and *Blanche* of Orleans. — Grand-Duchess of Tuscany. — Prince *Orloff* from Russia.

1864. *Amelia,* Queen of Saxony. — Donna *Maria* of Portugal, Duchess of Saxony. — Count and Count-

*) The numbers of distinguished persons, who together with those belonging to the middle and lower classes, made a pilgrimage to Einsiedeln in 1861, being extraordinarily great, it has been impossible to do more than give a selection of a few of the most widely known names.

In the year

ess *Montalembert.* — Lord *Dunraven* from Ireland. — Marquis of *Bethune* with his family.

1865. The Duke of Norfolk.

1866. Archbishop *Merode,* Almoner of Pius IX. — Mgr. *Dupanloup,* Bishop of Orleans. — Mgr. *Nardi,* domestic Chaplain to Pius IX. — Prince and Princess *Borghese* with their family. — *Frances,* Princess of Joinville. — The Duchess of Chartres.

1867. The Archbishops and Bishops of St. Francisco, St. Louis, Cincinnati and many other Prelates. — Four members of the Japanese embassy at Paris.

1868. The Queen of Naples.

1869. Mgr. *Dupanloup,* Bishop of Orleans. — Dr. *Augustus Theiner,* Librarian at the Vatican.

1870. Archbishop *Spalding* of Baltimore. — Bishops *Serra* from Australia and *Sweeny* from New-Brunswick. — Princes of Thurn and Taxis.

1871. A great number of Prelates, among whom may be named Mgr. *Dupanloup* and Mgr. *Mermillod.* — *Henry,* Archduke of Austria and his family. — Duke *Salviati* from Rome. — The Duke of Norfolk. — Marquis *Patrizi* from Rome. — Count *Charles Bodenham* with his wife from England. — Earl of Denbigh from England.

1872. *George,* Prince of Prussia. — Countess *Montalembert.* — Countess *Merode.*

1873. Archbishop *Vaughan* from Sydney. — Mgr. *Dupanloup.*

1874. Bishop *Ignatius Ordonez* of Riobamba in the Republic of Ecuador. — Prince and Princess *Radziwill.* — *Marie,* Queen of Saxony.

1875. Mgr. *Dupanloup.* — Earl of Denbigh.

In the year

1877. Archbishop *Paul Melchers* of Cologne. — Mgr. *Dupanloup.*

1878. Archbishop *Langenieux* of Rheims. — Mgr. *Dupanloup* of Orleans. — Mgr. *Bagnoud* of Bethlehem, Abbot of St. Maurice in Canton Valais, Switzerland.

1880. Mgr. *Machelbeuf,* Vicar apostolic of Colorado. — Abbot *Horner* of St. Peters at Salzburg. — *Louis,* Duke of Nemours. — Archduke *Henry* with his wife and family. — Prince *Jerome Napoleon.* — The Princess of Fürstenberg. — The Princes *Czartoryski,* &c.

1881. Count *Albert* of Thun. — Dowager, Duchess of Norfolk, and the Ladies *Howard.* — *Henry,* Count of Chambord. — Mgrs. *Freppel* and *Ratisbon* of Angers and about 200 French Priests.

The names selected from the lists in the Monastery books are those most likely to be familiar to general readers, they are however but a tithe of the numbers who have made the pilgrimage to Einsiedeln.

As has already been mentioned, the average yearly number of Communions at Einsiedeln, during the last three hundred years, has been 150,000. In the year 1710 it rose to 260,940, and in the year 1749 to 226,500. During the French revolution the influx of pilgrims, especially from France, was very great.

In the year of the Jubilee, 1861, the Communions were over 210,000.

One of the most interesting events connected with the pilgrimage, is the resort thither in the year 1864 of the Parish of St. Laurence in Paris. Three hundred and fifty of the Faithful, attended by sixty five Priests, belonging to Paris and its environs, set out under the guidance of the venerable Curé M. l'Abbé Duquesnay on Sunday, the 12th of June, after Mass, for the terminus of the Eastern Railway and were accompanied to the Station by their relations and friends.

Twenty five hours later they entered Einsiedeln in thirty five large vehicles, singing hymns and chanting sacred canticles. Amid the melodious pealing of bells, they went in procession up the great stone steps into the Church, and after having made their act of thanksgiving, betook themselves to the various guest-houses with which the town abounds. The following day was consecrated to the exercises of the Pilgrimage. The next morning, filled with joy and gratitude the pilgrims started on their return journey to their homes.

Numerous as are the pilgrimages made throughout the year to the Sanctuary of Our Lady of the Hermits, it is on the 14th of September, the anniversary of the Feast of the Divine Dedication, that the vast proportions of the Church are found all too small for the crowds of people who flock thither. Of one of these anniversaries Viscount de

Melun gives the following most interesting account: „Einsiedeln was more animated than on the occasion of my previous visit at an earlier period of the year. The approach of the festival infused into it glad life and activity; along all the roads leading to the village pilgrims were advancing towards the Sanctuary, the guest-houses and the streets were crowded, and on the eve of the 14th there was no room left in the little town for the numbers that were still flocking thither. The people, wandering from the Church to the surrounding heights, or scattered over all the open spaces and the avenues leading to the town, resembled a camp composed of a hundred different nations and a thousand tribes. The variety of costume and of physionomy revealed at a glance the most opposite habits and manners, the gravity of Germany contrasted with the vivacity of Italy; while each Canton had its own characteristics, and each family its favourite prayers, but all were animated by one and the same motive, only the country, age and sex of each varied in the expression of it. France also, indifferent as she is said to be to the ancient Faith, had sent some few of her children, some peasants, some old soldiers &c. who still believe in the omnipotence of God, and who, amidst wars and revolutions, have not forgotten their prayers. I recall to mind with emotion, a poor man who had come from the farthest parts of Alsace, bringing his poor blind wife with him to Einsiedeln, and above all the touching accents of their gratitude for the too slight alms bestowed on them by their compatriot, and their wishes that my family might long continue to enjoy the blessing of sight. Touching wishes from such as have been deprived of it!

The whole of the day was devoted to pious offices, preludes of the festival about to be celebrated. Little by little the Church filled, and at Vespers it was difficult to penetrate thro' the crowds, which were so pious and recollected that not a single word mingled with the chanting of the psalms, not a movement of curiosity disturbed the order of the ceremonies. After vespers the Monks returned to the penitentiary to resume their places in the confessionals, which had been besieged since the morning, just in the same manner as places of amusement are thronged elsewhere. The great candles and nearly all the lamps were extinguished, except those burning before the Blessed Sacrament and in front of the Statue of Our Lady of the Hermits. The Church had been given up to darkness and prayers were being recited aloud by the pilgrims. From every part of the vast edifice, from every side Chapel and from every bench arose a murmured sound

of prayer creating a most marvellous impression
of which no words can convey any idea; it was
the united voice of all who had come to Einsiedeln
to celebrate the festival of Our Lady of the
Hermits; it was the expression of the longing
desires, of the innermost feelings of ten thousand
pilgrims; accents of sorrow and of hope, psalms
of thanksgiving for a miracle, sighs and entreaties
that one might be performed, a Te Deum and a
Stabat, groans of penitence, expressions of ardent
love, the prayer of the Publican, the appeal of
the Centurion, the cry of the Leper, the tears of
the Magdalen; all that in the days of the gospel
the Saviour had listened to from suppliant humanity; all that the human soul can say to and
ask from God, *all* was to be heard in that strange
and supernatural murmur.

Although night was quickly advancing, I could
not bear to leave the Church, or separate myself
from my brethren; I felt as though their simple
and recollected souls lifted me upwards on the
wings of their desires and their merits, and that
whilst they commended themselves and all whom
they loved best on earth to the care of the
Mother of God, they included me, their un-
known brother, in their supplications, compensa-
ting for my unworthiness, thanks to the holy
union foretold in the gospel. I was enjoying

one of those privileged hours, one of those moments of grace in which God can refuse nothing to prayer. I was continually finding something fresh to ask for my relatives and for my friends. Alas! perhaps I shall never again hear voices so pure and so expressive!

It was, however, necessary to think of repose, but still the wonderful sound of united prayer, to which I had been listening, accompanied me to my retreat, and for a long time after sleep had weighed heavily on my eyelids, I still heard its voice, like to that of a mother singing her infant to rest.

On the day of the festival the Chapel of the Blessed Virgin was brilliantly illuminated. As early as four o'clock Masses began to be said at all the altars; the Bread of Angels was distributed to the Faithful, and the Abbot offered the Holy Sacrifice for the people. At ten o'clock the Papal Nuncio officiated pontifically; the arches resounded with the sacred music which so well expresses the aspirations of the heart, gladness was depicted on every countenance, for recollection did not exclude joy, the consciences of all present having been reconciled to God and, with few exceptions, all having approached the Holy Table.

What a contrast to the amusements offered in our towns; to the pleasures that corrupt, to the

excesses which kill! A gentle and sweet gaiety
had descended upon all, charity was the soul of
their intercourse, every repast was preceded and
followed by prayer, it was the great family celebrating the festival of its mother, happy in her
presence and beneath her protection.

In the evening there was a solemn procession.
The Abbot, assisted by numerous priests, came
to take the Blessed Sacrament from the altar, and
preceded by the whole of his Religious, advanced
processionally between the ranks of the kneeling
multitude.

When he descended the steps of the Church,
bearing beneath a däis the God-made man, the
sky was covered with clouds, the darkness was
profound, nothing could be seen of the Monastery,
except a fiery cross, and the reflection through
the windows of the lamps burning before the
altar. The immense space in front of the Church
which, but a moment before, was quite empty
had disappeared beneath the flood of pilgrims
whilst the long file of monks, each with a
lighted taper in his hand, described a moving
and luminous line through the multitudes.

Great flaming torches revealed here and there
groups of people in reverential attitudes and with
recollected demeanour. The Reposoir was erected
at the opposite end of the space facing the Church;

its pillars, its arched roof, and the altar and tabernacle were marked out with lines of fire, and
the Blessed Virgin in like manner, as St. John
beheld her, with the crescent beneath her feet
and crowned with stars, presented her Son to
the veneration of the world.

Beyond and above the illuminated town the
distant alps projected their giant forms against
the sky. The wind, sweeping from the glaciers,
bowed down the lofty pine trees in lowly homage
to the Divine Majesty and mingled its grave and
majestic murmur with the boom of the cannon,
the pealing of the bells, the sighs of the organ
and the chants of the priests and the people.

Arrived at the Reposoir, the Abbot intoned
those beautiful Eucharistic hymns which were composed by saints and are repeated by the angels,
after which he turned to the people to give the
blessing. All was then silence and attention;
every forehead was bowed to the ground, every
soul was raised to heaven, none prayed any longer, but every one adored, and at the moment
when, at the voice of the Priest, the Trinity
Itself blessed us from the supernal heights revealed by Faith, the Pilgrims of Einsiedeln believed that they beheld Our Lady of the Hermits
graciously and with smiles receiving their homage
whilst each one of them heard a voice in the

depths of his heart assuring him that his prayer
was sucessful and that the object of his pilgrimage
was accomplished.

Whenever the 14th of September falls on a
Sunday, the celebration of the festival continues
throughout the week, and on each day is observed with the utmost solemnity and pomp: on
these occasions the influx of Pilgrims is even
greater than in ordinary years; it is impossible to
find sufficient accommodation in the town, and
the neighbouring villages as well as the portion
of the Monastery set apart for guests, and even
the Church itself, are filled each night to overflowing.

As the foundation of the Pilgrimage to Our
Lady of the Hermits goes back to the 9th century,
the ancient Abbey of Einsiedeln celebrated on
the 21st January 1861 the thousandth anniversary
of St. Meinrad.   For a long time previously Einsiedeln had been preparing for the celebration
of its Jubilee.   The whole of the surrounding
population was united in the resolve that nothing
should be wanting to the public expression of
its gladness, and that the pilgrims, no matter
how numerous they might be, should receive a
cordial reception.   The Monastery had spared
nothing in order to give unaccustomed pomp to
the religious solemnities of the festival, and such

splendour as should be in accordance with the general anticipation. The restoration of the Choir, undertaken some years before at great expense, had at last been finished. The whole of the Church, and especially the Holy Chapel, was decorated with exquisite taste. The programme of the festival had been published in foreign journals and an extraordinary influx of pilgrims arrived on the 14th and the 29th of September and on the 13th of October. These dates are famous in the history of the Sanctuary, the 14th of September being the anniversary of the Divine Dedication of the Holy Chapel, the 29th of the same month that of the translation of the Holy Statue from the Vorarlberg to Einsiedeln in 1803, and the 13th of October that of the translation of the relics of St. Meinrad from Reichenau to the Chapel of Our Lady of the Hermits in 1039.

A large majority of the Pilgrims in 1861 belonged to the highest classes of society in Switzerland, France, Germany, Italy &c. and Princes and Princesses and many illustrious personages then presented on the holy mountain the touching spectacle of a lively faith and of a tender devotion towards the august Mother of God.

In proportion as the pilgrimage to Our Lady of the Hermits increases year by year, thanks in some measure to the extension of railways

and the means of communication which did not
exist in earlier times, and also in proportion to
its true nature being better known and more
highly appreciated, the Monastery, which fulfils a
large portion of its mission by consecrating itself
to the spiritual needs of the Pilgrims, receives
from all sides, proofs of veneration and esteem.

The roads which, for more than a thousand
years, have led to the Sanctuary in the „dark
wood" are at the present day more frequented
than ever.   Pilgrims find their way thither from
all parts of the earth and it is easy to understand the impossibility of preserving complete
lists of their names. As to the Monastery, it has
never been in so flourishing a state, never has
its sphere of influence been so widely extended,
or the number of its members so considerable,
never has its energy and activity been displayed
in so many different directions, never has it received more distinguished marks of approbation,
never has it been so well known in distant countries, as it is now.

These striking facts must lead the reader to
ask himself the question — what are the motives
and the objects which draw so many to Einsiedeln.
It is impossible that deception and illusion should
be the cause of so general and lasting a practice.
Illusions vanish with the lapse of time, but the

Pilgrimage to Einsiedeln has continued and increased through many succeeding centuries. The
earlier pilgrims must have found and experienced
something there, the thankful remembrance of which
they not only retained themselves, but transmitted
to their children and their children's children. It
is, therefore, the experience of miracles worked
and of favours received at the shrine of Our
Lady of the Hermits, which still attracts pilgrims
of all classes and all countries to a spot consecrated by the faith of past generations. It would
be easy to cite a great number of miracles
clearly proving the predilection of Our Holy
Mother for her Sanctuary of the Hermits, but
they are facts so generally known to people of
different countries that it is not necessary to give
them in detail.

The object which the Pilgrim has in view is
best declared by his actions. Disengaged for a
short time from domestic cares, he occupies himself solely with spiritual interests, to which he has
consecrated the whole of his leisure. The salvation of his soul is the one object which he has
in view, and which enables him to bear, cheer-
fully and patiently, all the discomforts of his
pilgrimage. Repentance for past sins, reconcili-
ation with God, the renewal and strengthening
of every virtue and of fidelity to duty are the

aims he sets before him — if he also asks for
temporal graces he makes them a matter of
secondary importance.

In all classes and conditions of men sorrows
are to be found which need consolation, secrets
of conscience which demand extraordinary counsel and burdens of the spirit which crave for
special help — such particular consolation, such
special grace, such profound counsel are granted
by the Divine Spirit on these occasions. The
Pilgrim starts on a laborious journey to seek
at the feet of the Blessed Virgin for that peace
of heart and divine strength which he so sorely
needs.

The Pilgrimage itself offers a multitude of cir-
cumstances calculated to reanimate Faith. The
suspension of daily duties and occupations, the
parting from home, the solitude of the road, its
difficulties and roughnesses, the soul elevating
majesty of the lofty, snow - crowned Alps, the
splendid and beautiful Monastery Church, the solemnity of the functions, the magnetism of the
mental union of so many persons of different
nations, but of one Faith — these and many other
causes aid the Pilgrim to self examination, isolating
him from worldly things, opening his whole being
to the Spiritual, intensifying his desires for holiness and virtue and for all that unites him to

God. The recollection also of the power of
the Blessed Virgin to succour all who seek her
help, and of the love between Jesus and His
Mother, further feeds and rests the heart of the
Pilgrim at Einsiedeln, where her protection is
specially vouchsafed. The Religious house, its
venerable age, and striking history, the divinely
consecrated Chapel, the miracles performed there,
and the graces obtained — all these are consider-
ations calculated to make a great and abiding
impression on the soul.

No reasonable friend of humanity can, therefore, find fault with the pilgrimage, but if uncon-
vinced of its utility, then let him determine to
judge for himself and instead of preventing others
from going there, let him accompany them to
Einsiedeln.

This description cannot be more appropriately
concluded than by quoting the opinions entertained of Einsiedeln by two illustrious men, one
of whom is almost a pagan, while the other is
a canonised Saint. It is thus that Goethe expresses himself in his memoirs: „The antique
dwelling of St. Meinrad, he says, appeared to me
something extraordinary of which I had never
seen the like. The sight of the little building,
surrounded by great pillars and surmounted by
arches, excited in me serious reflections. It is

there that one single spark of holiness and the fear of God kindled a flame which is always burning, and which has never ceased to give light; a flame to which faithful souls make a pilgrimage, often attended with great difficulties, in order to kindle their little taper at its holy flame. It is such a circumstance as this which makes us understand that the human race stands in infinite need of the same Light and the same heat which the first anchorite who inhabited this spot nourished and enjoyed in the depths of his soul, animated as it was by the most perfect faith."

St. Charles Borromeo on his side, gives similar testimony. Writing to his cousin the Cardinal of Hohen-Ems in 1576 he says: „I have a hundred things to tell you about my journey and yet I shall only mention one, namely my visit to the Sanctuary of Our Lady of the Hermits, of which I must say that next to the Holy House of Loretto, said to have been transported from under other skies by the hands of angels, I know of no place where my soul has been inflamed with such pious ardour as it was at Einsiedeln."

Chapter VIII.

The Village of Einsiedeln.

THE large and flourishing village of Einsiedeln
stretches down from the Monastery to the little
river Alp, and is the principal place in the district known by the same name. The parish comprises the outlying villages of Bennau, Egg,
Willerzell, Gross, Euthal and Trachslau, the
Commune numbering 8403 souls, and the village
of Einsiedeln proper, 4266.

The village is divided into two almost equal
portions by a paved street, and is situated in a
pleasant valley enclosed by two ranges of mountains of moderate height. Additions are constantly being made to it, and during the last few
years it has been greatly improved and beautified.
From the surrounding heights, which are easy
of ascent, beautiful views are to be obtained of
the Cantons of St. Gall, Zurich &c., and of the
snow-clad Alps which bound the horizon.

The botanist will find in the neighbourhood many rare plants, and the geologist many different kinds of minerals, together with a rich booty in fossils.

Between the village and the Monastery lies the spacious „Place" which has already been mentioned. It is almost surrounded by shops, stalls and booths, which are filled with books of devotion, statues, pictures and articles of piety intended as souvenirs of the pilgrimage. In the centre of the „Place" is the fountain of the Bles-

sed Virgin, constructed of grey marble, and whose
pure sparkling waters flow through fourteen bronze
pipes. Pilgrims may often be seen there slaking
their thirst and bathing their faces. On the
fountain is placed a beautiful bronze statue of
Mary Immaculate, and over it, ·resting on seven
pillars is a lofty and majestic baldaquin supporting
a golden crown. Beyond the fountain are the
great stone steps with arcades leading up to
the Monastery which forms the boundary of the
Place on the South.

When the sun is shining brightly the immense
façade, pierced by no less than a hundred windows, resembles a mirror with thousands of facets
which sparkle and reflect their light upon the
Place and the fountain in its midst.

The village of Einsiedeln has given many
distinguished men to the forest Canton of Schwytz,
among whom may be named the Prince Abbot
Placidus Reymann (1629—1670), beneath whose
rule the Monastery flourished exceedingly, and
rose high in public esteem. The Emperor bestowed on him the dignity of Count and the
Pope, during the wars which broke out whilst he
was ruling over the Abbey, commended him and
the Monastery in an especial manner to the protection of France and Austria. He also caused
the functions of the Church to be celebrated

with hitherto unwonted pomp, added fresh buildings to the Convent and increased the Library by many costly folios which are still marked with his coat of arms.

Amongst the scientific men who were natives of Einsiedeln one of them, a physician and chemist of great-renown, Theophrastus Paracelsus von Hohenheim by name, was born there in 1493 and died at Salzburg in 1541. He was the author of many theological as well as medical works, and also of a great number of treatises on philosophy. In consequence of his advanced knowledge of the natural sciences the common people believed him to be a sorcerer.

Brother Kuriger of Einsiedeln was distinguished as an artist and especially as a modeller in wax and clay. At the beginning of the present century his productions, finding their way into foreign countries, were greatly esteemed, especially at Vienna and Paris.

Wikart also practised the same branch of art. His anatomical tables, modelled in clay, which are preserved in the Natural History collections of the Monastery, are a remarkable proof of his thorough knowledge and of his technical skill.

A sculptor in wood and stone, Bodenmüller also made a name for himself, as did Birchler, who was a clever portrait painter.

The inhabitants of Einsiedeln are distinguished
for their lively, genial disposition and the richness of
the faculties with which they are endowed. A large
proportion of the population is engaged in the
breeding of cattle and in agriculture; the cows and
horses of the so-called Einsiedeln stock being the
most excellent of the famed Swiss breeds. Their
principal source of revenue is, however, the Pilgrimage. The village contains upwards of a
hundred large guest-houses, as well as numerous
smaller ones where Pilgrims are received. Many
of the former are provided with all the comforts to
be found in modern Hotels, whilst the houses set
apart for the lowest classes of Pilgrims are clean
and suitably furnished. Another branch of industry which employs a portion of the inhabitants
is a waxbleaching manufactory. There are also
two cotton manufactories, and a good deal of silk
weaving is carried on in the district, hand-looms
being in use in many of the cottages. Lastly, Einsiedeln, for a long time past, has distinguished itself
through its establishments devoted to the higher
branches of industry and art. Thus there are no
less than three houses of this kind in the village,
the most important of which is the celebrated firm
of CHARLES AND NICHOLAS BENZIGER BROTHERS.
This establishment alone comprises a typographic
printing office of 20 presses aided by type-setting,

electro-typing and a stereo foundry. A chromo-
lithographic printing office of 18 presses, a copper-
plate printing office of 7 presses and a large book
bindery of over 40 presses also belong to the
firm. Moreover, it possesses photographic, photo-
zinkographic and xylographic studios, where a
large number of artists are engaged in the pro-
duction of religious pictures. Mess[rs] Benziger also
own two large book-binding establishments at
Euthal and Gross. This business, some houses
of which are situated on the square opposite the
Monastery, was founded in the year 1792, and
has ever since steadily developed, so that it is
now spread not only over Europe, but also possesses three establishments in America, at New-
York, Cincinnati and St. Louis. In one of the
above-mentioned houses on the square, are the
extensive magazines for the sale of prayer-books
and books of devotion in German, English, French,
Italian, Spanish and other languages. The firm
also publishes handsome illustrated works, books
suitable for family reading, for children, and for
the people, school books, and ecclesiastical compositions. Since the year 1867, Mess[rs] Benziger
have edited an illustrated fortnightly magazine
entitled « *The old and the new World*», which is
widely circulated in Europe and America. The
modelling of casts, the manufacture of rosaries,

ESTABLISHMENTS FOR GRAPHIC ARTS.

CHARLES & NICHOLAS BENZIGER BROS. EINSIEDELN SWITZERLAND.

crucifixes, medals and other objects of piety, and in America the extensive manufacture of church vestments and holy vessels, claim a large portion of the attention of the firm. The number of people employed in it amounts to 700; besides a large number of artists at Einsiedeln and in nearly all the great european cities who are constantly at work for their litterary and artistical enterprises.

Everybody who pays a visit to these most interesting establishments, which no tourist should omit to do, must be struck how a business of this description could be carried on with such success in a village so far remote from all the great centres of literature and art. Also the merits of the firm have not only been recognized in the most flattering manner at several international exhibitions, but by a special favour, the late Pope Pius IX, honoured Charles and Nicholas Benziger Brothers by granting them the official title of *Typographers to the Holy See.*

It is not to be expected that a village like Einsiedeln should have many public buildings. There are, however, two, which call for remark; namely, the new and commodious School with the children's chapel, containing a beautiful altarpiece by Deschwanden, and the more recently erected Hospital.

CHAPTER IX.

The Neighbourhood of Einsiedeln.

THE Pilgrim having made acquaintance with
the Monastery and the Village will do well to
cast a glance on the objects of interest to be
found in the environs, before he returns to
his home.

First let him direct his steps to the South,
and after half an hour's walk thro' pleasant meadows and along the valley of the Alp, at the end
of which rise the majestic peaks of the Mythen,
he will perceive a humble *Convent of Benedictine
Nuns*, situated on the slope of the mountain to
his right. The Convent owes its origin to some
pious maidens who in the year 1200, were attracted by devotion for the Blessed Virgin to
Einsiedeln. In a valley of the forest of the Alp-
egg they made for themselves little separate
dwellings, where they lived under a Superior and
were known by the name of „Sisters of the Forest".

About the year 1403 a charitable person of the
name of Grätzer having bestowed on them a piece
of ground, they built a Convent on the site where
the present one stands, and dwelt there under the
protection of the Monastery of Einsiedeln. A
conflagration having destroyed a large portion of
their house, the poor sisters, despite their poverty,
succeeded in building another house by means of
alms which they received from Germany. In the
year 1602 Prince Abbot Augustine I. rebuilt
their convent and placed them under the rule
of St. Benedict. Up to that time they had
had no chaplain living at their Convent, and had
therefore been obliged, summer and winter, to
assist at the offices at the Monastery Church, which
was no easy matter when summer heat and
winter cold had to be encountered, making of
their daily journey, a true pilgrimage. But when
their new Convent was built the Abbot Augustine
provided them with a Chaplain and appointed
one of his Benedictine Fathers their Director.
In 1798 the poor and pious Nuns shared in the
fate which befell the Monastery, and were obliged
to exchange their beloved solitude for the miseries
of a forced exile which lasted several years.

Numerous postulants have of late continued
to present themselves at the Convent, being attracted thither by the special devotion to which

The Convent of the Benedictine Nuns near Einsiedeln.

the Nuns consecrate themselves, namely, the perpetual Adoration of the Blessed Sacrament. By day and night the Chapel resounds with the prayers and canticles which the Sisters unceasingly offer to Almighty God in union with the great Propitiatory Sacrifice perpetually offered on the altars. A large number of Pilgrims, and of persons living in the world are aggregated to this work of reparation, in order that they may profit by its graces.

In the year 1880 the Convent-Chapel was pulled down, as being too small and inconvenient, and the Nuns have now built a more commodious one. As they have few possessions, and no resources to fall back upon they are obliged to gain a livelihood by making and embroidering vestments. This work is performed in such a skilful and beautiful style that it is a pity the excellence they have attained in this branch of industry should not be more generally known. The poor Sisters are often without orders, as is the case at present, when specially in need of means not only for self-support but for paying off the debt on their Church. It is, not however in the making of vestments alone that the Nuns are employed, they are obliged even to work in the fields which adjoin their Convent and to attend to their cattle and perform all kinds of menial work. Despite the smallness of their means they share them with the poor and no one is sent away from the Convent without a basin of soup and bread. So perfectly do these good Sisters practise the law of charity to God and man that they are held in the highest possible esteem throughout the whole district, and are blessed alike by God and by their neighbour.

Turning his steps to the North from Einsiedeln, and proceeding on the road to Rapperswyl, the Pilgrim will in process of time reach the *Chapel of St. Meinrad,* on the heights of the Etzel. Year after year pilgrims flock there in thousands to pray, and venerate the saint whose history is depicted on the altar-piece and on the frescos of the roof.

Between Einsiedeln and the Etzel the wayfarer, on descending the hill, will come to the Sihl, a wild mountain torrent, which flows tumultuously along its wild and rocky bed. The solid stone bridge by which it is spanned was constructed 600 years ago under the direction of one of the lay-brothers of Einsiedeln, and has been rebuilt during the present century. In the neighbourhood of this bridge the house still exists in which Theophrastus Paracelsus was born. From the Sihl bridge, which, in common with many other bridges stretching boldly across a mountain torrent, is known by the name of the Devil's bridge, the road passes for a long while between tree- less barren moors out of which turf is dug and laboriously prepared for fuel. Soon, however, the eye is again rejoiced by the sight of green fields, here and there crowned with dark pine forests. To the East a glimpse is obtained of the picturesque valley of the Sihl which is about two hours distant from Einsiedeln. The lofty mountains enclosing the green valley on three sides form the buttresses of the majestic alpine chain of the Glärnisch mountains, the highest being the Great and Little-Fluhbrig (called by the peasants „Diethelm") and at the foot of their sharply hewn perpendicular walls the Sihl has its source.

Lastly, if the Pilgrim turn his eyes to the heights on the West of Einsiedeln he will see a building which owes its creation to the noblest christian charity. It is an Orphanage for boys on the mountain called Maria-End, founded in 1869 by Counsellor Stephen Steinauer-Benziger, who was, alas, too early called away from the scene of his earthly labours in the year 1878. He also erected the beautiful little Chapel set apart for the inmates. The institution contains about 30 orphans who are trained and educated under the care of a priest and several sisters. On visiting it the pilgrim will surely pray that it

Mount Etzel.

may please God to bless so beautiful a good work and give it long life and prosperity.

Receive my greetings, woods of pine and beech!
Sweet scents of Alpine flowers perfume the air,
And jubilant rings out the song of birds,
Of saucy chaffinch and of blackbird staid.
Oh lovely hills! from out the narrow vale
Lift me that I may breathe the clear pure air,
And thence, amidst the herbage-covered heights,
Gaze down upon the verdant pastoral land!

* * *

See! in the very centre of the vale
The buildings of the noble cloister stand
Neath clustering roofs, which like a forest seem;
Into the sky two towers uplift their Domes,
And in the sunbeams shines the golden cross;
Whilst, deeper lying in the beauteous Au,
Crowded together or in scattered groups
The thickly-peopled village stretches out.

P. Gall Morel.

CHAPTER X.

Personal Recollections.

A never-to be-forgotten day was that on which B. and I set out for Einsiedeln. It was a lovely afternoon in the beginning of July, the sun was shining brightly as we left Ragatz and the sky was blue as a turquoise; all nature seemed to be rejoicing in the pleasant light and genial heat of the midsummer season.

At Wädensweil we seated ourselves in the train which takes the traveller by the mountain railway to Einsiedeln, and as we slowly ascended, the views on either side of us became more beautiful. Below us to our left was the bright shining Lake, whilst on our right were green, picturesque, Alpine dells, pine forests, mountain torrents, and, in front of us, far away, on the horizon, the serrated peaks of the Churfirsten range rose into the azure sky. After passing for a little while along a narrow defile, suddenly, at a most pic-

turesque turn of the road, we came in sight of
the goal of our pilgrimage. In the midst of a
long valley, closed at the further end by the
grand forms of the larger and smaller Mythen,
appeared the Monastery, encased, like a precious
jewel, in a setting of verdant slopes and lofty
fir-clad heights. In the centre rose the noble
Church with its two majestic towers, the great
grey piles of the Monastery buildings stretching
out on either side, and their innumerable windows
glittering like diamonds in the rays of the setting
sun. One glance was sufficient to make us feel
that high as our expectations had been raised,
they were not destined to be disappointed.

The impression which had been made upon
us, when first the Abbey disclosed itself so suddenly to our view, was deepened and strengthened
in proportion as we drew nearer and nearer to
it, until from the windows of our Hotel we could
study it at leisure. Immediately before us lay
the large irregular Place flanked by guest-
houses, the „St. Catharine" the „St. Joseph"
and the „Three Kings"; whilst from the centre
of it rose the gleaming fountain of Our Blessed
Lady with her statue under its sheltering canopy
and glittering crown, whilst below it streams of
water, pouring incessantly into their channel,
sparkled and flashed perpetually. In the little

The valley of Einsiedeln.

shops, at the doors of the booths, and on
either side of the great steps leading up to the
Church, women were sitting, their nimble fingers
busily engaged in making rosaries of all kinds
of beads and seeds which they were manufacturing
in such quantities that is was impossible to believe
sufficient purchasers would ever be found for them.

Beyond the Place, and situated on a wide
platform above it, the Monastery rose in its simple
grandeur and not many minutes passed ere we
were quickly ascending the steps and entering
the Church by one of its side portals.   But the
air within was so cold in contrast to that which
I had been breathing outside that I dare only
linger a moment before the Holy Chapel and take
one hasty glance at the vast interior of the sacred
building.   I had been told that I should think
it gaudy, but it is sober in colouring compared
with the generality of Italian Churches.   For the
thousands of pilgrims who visit it year after year
the frescos with which it is so profusely adorned
form a perfect Bible, teaching them lessons which
they will never afterwards forget, whilst the rich
decorations of every portion, and the heavenly
cheerfulness which is its distinguishing characteristic must make many of the innumerable poor
who flock thither to pray and to praise God, feel
as though Paradise itself had come down to

earth, enabling them to realise, as they never could have done before, that the House of God is in truth the Gate of Heaven. Happy indeed, and abiding, must be the impression received by them when, after their long and weary pilgrimage they are suddenly ushered into such a Temple!

Before four o' clock the next morning I was roused by the sound of a bell, giving evidence that the Masses had begun at the Church. Across the little green in front of my window groups of men and women were passing on their way thither, their prayer-books and rosaries in their hands, thankful to have it in their power to begin their day by assisting at the Holy Sacrifice. I believe it may with truth be said that there is hardly a man, woman or child at Einsiedeln who is not present at one or other of the daily Masses unless disabled by illness. The parish Mass proper is said at half past five in the Chapel of the Rosary, but it is rather a distracting one at which to assist, for whilst it is going on the Rosary is said in a loud voice by all who are present. At its close Holy Communion is given and it is astonishing to see the numbers of those who daily partake of It, not only at this Mass but also at those which follow and precede. It is given until after nine or ten o' clock and sometimes even later.

The Conventual Mass is sung at a quarter
past seven and is a delightful function, having
just enough music to help the soul on its upward
path and none of a kind to disturb recollection.
The choir is principally composed of the pupils
belonging to the College, and it often seemed to
me as if the clear melodious strains of their young
voices could hardly be less sweet than that of
the angel host when they came to proclaim peace
on earth to men of good will. As soon as the
Conventual Mass is over, as well as after Vespers,
the Pilgrims who are present flock to one of the
side altars to have their rosaries, statues, prayer-
books, and other souvenirs of their pilgrimage
blessed by one of the Benedictine Fathers. At
first I used to wonder what the big valises and
baskets which I saw people bringing into the
Church could possibly contain, but the problem
was quickly solved when after Mass they at once
began to empty out their treasures and then to
carry them to the altar. Many of these souvenirs
were evidently intended for presents and very
amusing it was to see the purchase of them. For
instance a shyfaced youth would spend an hour
at a booth weighing the rival merits of a prayer-
book bound in violet velvet with silver clasps or
in green morocco with gold ones, while another
would be equally anxious and perplexed about

a rosary, it being easy to see in both cases, that the gift was intended for some beloved village maiden. One morning as B. and I were sitting near the Church door, we were quite touched as well as entertained at witnessing the pride and delight a poor ragged little fellow took in his possession of an ugly brown clay figure of Our Blessed Lady, gilded here and there, and looking more like a piece of gingei bread than anything artistic. His first aim was to attract our attention, and when he had succeeded in doing so he began gradually to disclose his treasure, as though he feared that the effect of a sudden view of it might be too much for our nerves. Then, after he had had it blessed, it was delightful to see him walking by his mother hugging his statue in his arms as proud as a king. Two or three times afterwards we saw them wandering about the village, the last time they were evidently setting out on their homeward pilgrimage, his beloved statue having of course been carefully packed away in the „hotte" his mother was carrying on her back. Many of the pilgrims from distant villages who come only for the day spend all their time in the Church, going out now and then to eat a morsel of bread. Before they take their final leave, late in the afternoon, they are as busy as

they can be packing up their purchases in a basket.
It is pleasant to see them thus employed and to
feel that they look on the sacred building, not
only as the House of God, but also as their
Father's Home, where they may occupy themselves in innocent employments as they would
in their own dwellings. I have visited the Church
at all hours, but never have I seen it destitute
of worshippers. All day long the voice of prayer
ascends to heaven as well as that of praise.

The weather was very hot during nearly the
whole of the two months we spent at Einsiedeln,
and as the only cool spot we had near to our
Hotel was in the shadow cast by the great Church,
it was our custom to betake ourselves there with
our camp stools, our books and our work early
in the morning, and sitting close by one of
the portals, to watch the people who were constantly streaming in and out. On one occasion I
remember that we suddenly heard the voice of
singing break the silence, and looking into the
Church saw a group of Pilgrims, old men and
maidens, young men and children standing before
the Holy Chapel and chanting canticles in honor
of the Blessed Virgin.

When the Count de Melun was at Einsiedeln
some years ago he witnessed an incident of the
same kind of which, in his interesting „Souvenir"

he gives the following description. „Whilst I was praying before one of the altars", he says, „the Church resounded with a hymn to the Blessed Virgin; never had I heard a more enchanting melody, and St. John in the Isle of Patmos could scarcely, I think, have listened to a more ravishing concert. It was fifty Tyrolese Pilgrims who were singing a hymn in honor of Our Lady of the Angels. They had arrived that evening, and on the next day were going to return to their homes taking with them the blessing of the Virgin of Einsiedeln! Their fatiguing journey had been undertaken for no other purpose than that of pouring out their heart's desires at the foot of her image, reciting their chaplets, singing a psalm of thanksgiving, and then returning home fortified by the bread of angels. Scarcely could we distinguish thro' the shades of evening, the frank honest faces of the Tyrolese, their picturesque costumes, and the tired forms of the women and children who had derived from their faith the strength necessary for so long a journey. Some old men, weary with the burden of life and the hardships incident to their pilgrimage mingled with the sonorous voices of their younger companions the deep sighs which are inspired by a near approach to the grave. More than one mother, who perhaps had left her son upon a

bed of suffering, united her plaintive accents of
supplication with the songs of joy and accompanied them with her tears." Of such sweet and
pleasant surprises as these we had many during
our sojourn in that hallowed spot.

At three o' clock in the afternoon the murmured sounds of prayer rise while vespers are
being said by the Fathers in the Monastery choir,
then, when the office is over, the Sons of St. Benedict come in their turn to pay their homage
to Our Lady of the Hermits, while the Pilgrims
in serried ranks kneel behind them. As soon as
the Salve Regina has been sung in the same
old world tones which for centuries has been
heard in the same place, the Fathers and their
pupils return in slow procession, with bent heads
and reverent demeanour, down the aisle between
the rows of pilgrims standing on either side, and
re-enter the Monastery. Immediately after the door
has closed behind them, the people gather round
the altar where their souvenirs of the pilgrimage
are blessed, and afterwards resume their prayers,
which are continued until long after darkness has
come on for it is not until a late hour that the
Church is closed.

One great comfort and pleasure which the
Catholic visitor to Einsiedeln enjoys is that it is
a spot which does not attract tourists, and that

all who meet together there are of one heart and of one mind. Here, at least, is never seen the unseemly lounging and staring and whispering which so painfully distract the worshipper in the Churches throughout Italy. All and each of those gathered together in the sacred building have come there for one sole purpose, and their devotion and recollection is something wonderful.

There is none of the excitement here which one often sees Italians indulge in, no audible sobbing, or extravagant gestures. Pilgrims come into the Church quietly, they pray quietly, they go to confession quietly, and quietly they return to their homes. Although the music performed at festivals and on Sundays is very beautiful, it is strictly ecclesiastical in character, quite devoid of anything florid, or operatic, and never mingled with the display of solo singing which in the present day is too often heard in Churches. Consequently there is nothing that appeals to the sensuous feelings of the pilgrims, while, at the same time, there is everything which is needed to soothe and calm the soul and to help it to maintain a spirit of recollection. Moreover, when it is remembered that the compositions which are generally performed at Einsiedeln are those of such masters as Leo, Durante, Caponi, Bach, Händel and Haydn, it is hardly necessary to add that the standard which the Fathers have set up is a very high one.

I have said that numbers of people are, at all hours of the day, praying in the Church, but, of course, the majority is to be found in front of the Holy Chapel. Although situated close to the entrance of the building, the quiet there is as great as it is in the vicinity of the high altar at the further end of the Church, and no loud noise of footsteps, or clanging of doors, or sound of greetings, or farewells, distract the worshippers; they never turn their heads, never cast a glance around, but are utterly absorbed in their prayers and devotions. If, perchance, any one who is not a Catholic enters the Church, a unit among the assembled crowd, he is so impressed by what he sees, that, unconsciously perhaps, his demeanour becomes reverent and befitting the holy place in which he finds himself.

From all that I witnessed during my stay at Einsiedeln, it is evident that the people who make the pilgrimage there require no adjuncts to excite their devotion, no splendid functions, no magnificent vestments, no long processions with banners streaming in the air amid the clang of bells. A simple low mass succeeded by a sermon satisfies them and after that stillness and silence. Hardly a day passes but a Pilgrimage from one or another place, more or less distant, arrives, sometimes in numbers varying from 1000 to 2000, sometimes composed of two or three dozen families only. On the second day of our sojourn as B. and I were sitting beside the mountain path which leads to the summit of the Etzel, we heard in the distance a sound of chanting, and presently, coming down between the green meadows, we saw a great company of people advancing, men, women and children in equal proportions. It was a very hot day so the men had taken of their coats while the women, holding up their umbrellas to protect them from the sun, looked like a host of gigantic mushrooms. As they passed by they scarcely turned their eyes towards us, but looked straight before them, chanting their litanies as they walked quietly along. Following in their wake, we observed them halt as soon as they drew near the village, the men to put on their coats, the Curé to vest himself in his cotta, and the flag-bearer to unfurl his banner. Then they proceeded along the road, and having reached the great Crucifix at the corner of the village green, the bells of the Church rang out a welcome, and one of the Fathers, preceded by a lay-brother carrying a banner came out to meet them. The two banners having touched in salutation, the Benedictine Father and the Curé, followed by the Pilgrims,

advanced towards the Church, and having entered
the great portal, opened wide to receive them,
they knelt on the pavement in front of the Holy
Chapel there to give thanks for having been
permitted to reach the goal of their pilgrimage;
and also to implore the intercession of Our Blessed
Mother to enable them to make good use of the
privileges they were about to enjoy.   Their whis-
pered petitions ended, they left the Church and
dispersed to seek in the various guest-houses the
rest and refreshment so sorely needed after the
labours of the day.

Some, however remained seated on the benches
outside the Church where they partook of the
food they had brought with them.   After resting
an hour or two they returned to the Church to
resume their devotions until Vespers.

The office being ended one of the Fathers
ascended the pulpit and preached for more than
an hour, to the great delight of the Pilgrims who
love long sermons, and their rapt attention was
most edifying. The sermon over, as many as could
crowd into the Penitentiary Chapel did so, and, as
soon as there was no longer any standing room
the door was closed, while those unable to get in
sat on the steps awaiting their turn. The Penitentiary, as has already been mentioned, is a spacious
building. Of the twenty eight confessionals ranged

on either side some are for the French, others for
Germans, others for Italians &c. One Benedictine
Father hears confessions in English, but alas! it
is seldom that one of our countrymen is seen
approaching his confessional. The Pilgrims remained praying until a late hour, for long after
dark I saw a faint light burning in the Church
showing that it was not yet emptied of its worshippers.

Some of the Pilgrimages are received with
more ceremony than others, in observance of
usages dating from far distant ages. Thus we observed that when the whole town of Rapperschwyl
with its syndic, the members of the municipality
and other officials at its head, made its annual
visit to Einsiedeln, all the Benedictine Fathers
issued from the Church to meet and welcome it,
preceded by the 200 pupils of the College clad
in soutane and cotta, bearing velvet cushions on
each of which reposed the relic of a Saint and
chanting litanies, while the bells of the Church
gave out their most melodious chimes

In the good old days now passed away, but
one would fain hope destined to return in God's
own time, the Pilgrimage from Schwytz, the capital
of the Canton, was marked by a really splendid
ceremonial, the Pilgrims being preceded by her-
alds to announce their approach, and the members

of the Governement being received with great pomp and solemnity.

As Our Lady of Mount Carmel is the Patron Saint of the parish of Einsiedeln, great numbers of people collected in the Church on the vigil of her Feast to assist at Vespers and to listen to the sermon that followed. On this occasion, as well as whenever there is a Pilgrimage to the shrine of Our Lady of the Hermits, it is very striking to see the men grouped about the various altars, men, for the most part between 20 and 45 years of age praying with wonderful fervour and recollection, each in his own language, and seeming as though he would take heaven by violence. The united sound of these numerous voices is like that of a mighty wind, rising through the shades of evening, and made an impression on me which I shall not easily forget.

In the gathering darkness the scene in the Church was most striking. Crowds of people surrounded the Holy Chapel, some kneeling and praying, some seated on the stone pavement reading by the light of little tapers which they held in their hand or stuck in the ground beside them. Small candles glimmered here and there in the nave where crowds of men were assembled, the only greater lights being those of the lamp before the Blessed Sacrament and those before Our

Lady of the Hermits. Many were obliged to remain in the Church through the night, there being no room for them in the guest-houses.

At three o' clock the following morning, when B. looked out from her window, she could see the faint light of tapers still glimmering in the Church as they had done when we had taken our last look at it the night before.

The numbers of Pilgrims visiting Einsiedeln on the Feast of the Assumption was greater far than even on the Feast of Our Lady of Mount Carmel. During the previous day, from early morning, people were streaming along the roads leading to the village, some coming from the direction of the Etzel, others along the valley which connects Einsiedeln with Schwytz and the Lake of Lucern, others crossing the mountains which separate it from the Lake of Zurich. None of the Pilgrims halted in the village; tired, foot-sore, and hungry, as they must many of them have been, they would not have felt satisfied and happy if, ere resting themselves, they had not first paid their homage in the Church before the Chapel of the Divine Consecration. Then, and not till then, did they begin to look out for lodgings wherein to spend the night. But, in spite of the hundred guest-houses and upwards, which the village contains their endeavours to find

accommodation were not all successful. At
our Hotel, which was filled from basement to
attics with guests of all ranks and positions in
life, from the noble to the peasant, fully a hundred
persons were rejected; and about fifty women
were obliged to pass the night in the Salles à
manger of the various Hotels. The day had been
a very rainy one, and many of the Pilgrims must
have been wet through, but not a sign of annoy-
ance was seen on any of their faces, old and
young, looked as happy and pleased as if they had
been favoured with the brightest and sunniest of
summer days. Rain was so much wanted for the
country, they said, how could they be otherwise
than glad and thankful? I forget how many thousands came to Einsiedeln on that occasion, but
I know that the Church holds eight thousand and
that it was so crowded from first thing in the
morning until after the last Mass was over that
there was scarcely standing room to be had.

On the evening of a previous day, when two
thousand people had made a Pilgrimage to Einsiedeln, a concert was given at our Hotel; the
musicians and singers being placed in the terrace
garden overlooking the great Place. It was
crowded from side to side with a vast multitude
of people, sitting or standing on the pavement,
and it was a curious sight to see the myriads

of faces turned up towards the spot whence the music proceeded, and looking of a waxen whiteness in the light cast upon them by the lamps set at intervals along the balcony.

On another occasion a concert was given by the Town Band of wind instruments in a small garden opposite the School, which was listened to with great delight by the peasants who chanced to have made a Pilgrimage to Einsiedeln on that day.

The village seems from time to time to have enjoyed many recreations. We have an account of one kind of them in an old diary dating from the year 1748. On the 4th of September Antonio Kälin, the Intendant, went to the Curé and recommended to his favorable notice an exhibition of Marionettes, requesting that the Proprietor might be allowed to show them at the Town Hall. Permission was given on the condition that the Curé should first inspect and pronounce upon the intended representation, and having done so the Marionettes were exhibited next day „after the Rosary" the performance lasting four hours.

Shooting at a target is also a very common amusement among the Swiss Youth „who form themselves into societies for that purpose" and hold their *tir*, as it is called, annually in different towns and villages. Whilst we were at Einsiedeln a *tir* took place there, and early one Sunday morning bands of young men came thither to have a shooting match which was held in a field adjoining the Monastery. A tent was erected there and flags placed at intervals on the green. Several men clad in scarlet stood at the targets to mark the shots, one of their number acting as Master of the Ceremonies. The match began at twelve o' clock and was over at five, when each company, preceded by its banner, departed in good order. The *tir* has, for many years past, been a favourite recreation with the people and more than one hundred years ago one of a very curious sort took place. On the 11th of July, the women of the village went forth from their houses, carrying banners, beating drums, and armed with pistols, their motive in doing so being to excite the astonishment of the men by their shooting. The standard-bearer was one Salome Kälin, still a common name at Einsiedeln, the Drum-Major being Carl Willi's shop girl. The Curé, it appears, had given them leave to close their shops whilst they were having their shooting match but, it is added by the relator of the story, they ought to have had a surgeon with them in case of any of them being wounded.

The various costumes to be seen at Einsiedeln

form an interesting feature of the pilgrimages. Among them the most common are those of the women from the Black Forest, whose head dresses are embroidered in gold and silver and furnished with two long black ribbons descending nearly to the feet. The prettiest costume is that of the peasants of the Vorarlberg, consisting of a skirt of black glossy material, trimmed half way up with a band of light blue braid; the bodice of black, or coloured velvet is embroidered in silver and gold, the patterns being always elegant and artistic; the narrow sleeves are of silk brocade, and on the head is worn a black straw hat, trimmed with bright ribbons and flowers. This costume is becoming even to old women, and for the young girls, who are generally pretty and have a sweet expression of countenance, it is especially suitable. There are also peasants who wear red handkerchiefs folded on their heads, and *gigot* sleeves, stuffed as full as pincushions at the shoulders; very short waists coming just beneath the arm-pits, and exceedingly short stuff petticoats, so closely plaited that they stand out some inches round the hips. Other women wear blue petticoats and black bodices over white linen chemisettes; the starched sleeves standing very high above the shoulders and reaching down as far as the elbows. Perhaps it is owing to the variety of

costume which the women of Einsiedeln are constantly in the habit of seeing, that many years
ago they were infected with such a love of
dress and delighted to wear such extraordinary
costumes „to their temporal injury and eternal
hurt", that the Curé, in order to turn them into
ridicule, caused a certain Ludwig Zing, a man
who was wont to act the part of fool during
the carnival, to parade the village dressed up in
the new Einsiedeln fashions, and especially to
caricature the fashionable head gear by deco-
rating his own with horns and bells.

The 14th of September, when the Feast of the
Divine Dedication is celebrated, is of course the
Day of Days at Einsiedeln. We were, alas!,
obliged to leave three weeks before it took place,
and a sad disappointment it was not to be able
to assist at it. As a proof of the impression
this Feast produces I may mention that a lady,
who has passed all her life in the village, and who
has never missed being present at one of these
anniversaries, told me that she felt on every suc-
cessive occasion, as though it were the first, so
deep and fresh was the impression made on her.
In every respect this festival is celebrated in a
far more splendid and solemn manner than that
of St. Meinrad, or Our Lady of the Hermits;
the Blessed Sacrament not being carried in pro-

cession round the great Place on either of those occasions as it is on the 14th of September. It is generally speaking only on that day that a French sermon is given, and it is hardly needful to add that it is always delivered by some Preacher of note.

From one of these sermons, preached by the Abbé Retours, the following extracts have been made, as they may serve to cast some fresh light on the signification of the Pilgrimage to Our Lady of the Hermits. „Although the whole earth belongs to the Lord," says the Abbé, „He has seen fit to choose certain spots in which more especially to show forth His mercy and goodness, communicating to them a sanctifying and healing influence, and manifesting Himself by the miracles which are at the root of all pilgrimages." Then alluding to the great festival which the people were engaged in celebrating, he exclaims: „Who is there among us who did not feel moved by the first solemn Mass said this morning in the Holy Chapel. Darkness reigned without, but already the Sanctuary was brilliantly illuminated and crowds of people were approaching the altar." Speaking of Einsiedeln itself he remarks that „it not only possesses, in a high degree, the sanctifying power to be found at all places of pilgrimage, but, on account

of the Patrons who are there honoured, it seems
to surpass every other shrine and to enjoy a
privilege possessed by itself alone. For it has
pleased the Almighty, he goes on to say, not only
to make it the place of His choice by means of
numerous and striking miracles, but also, through
an august consecration, to bestow on it a wonderful power of sanctification. In all pilgrimages
either the example set by a Saint, or his intercession is sought for, or the Protection of the
Blessed Virgin; and in the august and venerable
Sanctuaries of the Holy Land, we find the traces
of our Saviour's life and of the mysteries attached
to it. Now, by a miraculous privilege, granted to
Einsiedeln alone, these several characteristics are
found united together here. For this morning
whilst celebrating Mass in the Holy Chapel, what
had I before my eyes, but the venerated head
of the Holy Martyr St. Meinrad, and above it the
statue of Mary before which he delighted to pray,
whilst around me were the sacred walls consecrated a thousand years ago by the Saviour
and his angels. Thus surrounded, who could do
otherwise than believe that, when the Divine
Pontiff of the New Law touched with oil those
holy precincts, the angels must have repeated the
prayer which Solomon of old uttered on the day
of the consecration of the Temple of Jerusalem".

Alluding to St. Meinrad, the Abbé said that
„after longing during the whole of his existence
for a hidden life, and longing in vain, he must
surely have expected to find obscurity after
his death. But it was not so, for century after
century he was destined to be had in remembrance, and to have his memory for ever associated with the Pilgrimage to the splendid Church
of Einsiedeln".

Amongst the numerous pilgrims from distant
lands whom we met at our Hotel, was the venerable Abbé Carton who had come there to spend
the whole month of his yearly holiday, for, as he
said, it would take him all that time to get through
what he had to say to Our Blessed Lady of the
Hermits, and to plead with her to obtain for
him, I don't know how many thousand francs,
which he smilingly said his „bonne Mère" was
bound to procure, as she could not allow the
poor whom he had confided to her care, to remain any longer without the asylum he was
endeavouring to provide for them. It was to
this same Abbé Carton that on the 4th of August
1881, at the annual public sitting of the Académie
Française, a sum of 2000 francs was presented
by M. Ernest Renan, who also delivered a speech
in honour of his exertions in the cause of charity.

Shortly after we had left the place, Monseigneur

Freppel, Bishop of Angers, went to Einsiedeln
for the great festival of September the 14th, and
we may well imagine what must have been the
subject of his petitions as well as those of the
Count de Chambord who was also this summer
at Einsiedeln!

Yet another Pilgrim came to the Holy Chapel
not long ago, and prayed on his knees before
it, the tears pouring the while down his cheeks.
Surely this gives a grain of hope that he, on
whose eloquent accents all Paris once hung en-
raptured, may hereafter return to the fold from
whence he has strayed, there to find pardon
and peace.

The holy and venerable Bishop of Orleans,
Monseigneur Dupanloup, made frequent pilgrimages to Einsiedeln. The last time he was there
he told the Fathers he should return the next
year, for he had „so many things to ask of the
Blessed Virgin", but before the time he had fixed
upon had arrived, he was taken to Paradise, there
to intercede with his heavenly Mother, for his
beloved France more powerfully by far than he
could ever do on earth.

A very great pleasure it was to us whilst at
Einsiedeln to visit one of the Monks with whom
we had made acquaintance. On one of these
occasions he took us to the atelier where the

artist of the Community works at the pictures, altar-pieces &c. with which many of the neighbouring Churches are adorned. He is a disciple of Deschwanden, and there is a great resemblance between their works, those of the Monk manifesting the same religious feeling which was the chief characteristic of the Master. The Pictures of both involuntarily recall to memory the lovely creations of Fra Angelico, and no wonder, for like the great Dominican, Deschwanden never took pencil in hand without first addressing himself in prayer to God, and who can doubt that his example, in this respect, is followed by his disciple. Amongst the most remarkable of the Father's productions is one representing the stoning of St. Stephen, which we admired in a Church about two miles from Einsiedeln. When we had the pleasure of visiting him he was engaged upon a composition destined to be placed in the boy's college chapel, and in which are represented St. Cecilia as Patroness of music, St. Catharine of philosophy, St. Thomas Aquinas as Patron of theology, Fra Angelico of painting and St. Francis of poetry. This work will certainly be one of the most admirable and beautiful of any which the Artist has produced. He is not only a Painter, but a Musician also being, like many other of the Fathers, an able performer on the violin, and delighting to join in the trios and quartettes in which, from time to time, the Monks take their recreation. Among Protestants the idea seems generally to prevail that the life led in Monasteries must be either an idle, or a tiresomely monotonous one, but a visit to the Abbey of Einsiedeln would convince them that it is far from being so, and that in the Monasteries of the present day, as well as in those of the middle ages, of which such houses as that of Einsiedeln are but the continuation, the life led by the Monks is as full of variety and interest as any human existence possibly can be. Within its happy enclosure every talent is cultivated to the utmost, and each fills the position for which his abilities, the bent of his character, and his disposition best fit him. Actively employed during the whole day, either in researches connected with literature, the fine arts, philosophy, science or theology, or occupied in religious offices, in the confessional, the pulpit, or the College, or else engaged with the administration of the various possessions of the Monastery, every hour is filled up. The Monk then retires at eight o' clock in the evening to his cell, there to read in quiet, and resume, for as many hours as he pleases, the studies which have occupied him during the day.

Once during the year the Fathers go in parties of ten or twelve for a few days holiday to a country-house they have at Pfäffikon on the shores of the Lake of Zurich, immediately opposite to which is a picturesque island, also belonging to the Monastery, with a Church founded in 973. It was here, curious to say, that Ulrich von Hutten died, and was buried, in the year 1523. Close to the Church is a farm house surrounded by orchards, whence we once saw the Fathers bring a rich booty of rosy-cheeked apples on their return from their yearly excursion. They also, from time to time, visit their other dependencies, of which they have several in other parts of Switzerland, and on the borders of Austria. Of these various houses there is a series of water-colour drawings, in the gallery leading to the Abbot's apartments. Some of them are beautifully situated, several are large turreted buildings, having the air more of secular castles than of monastic establishments. Every now and then some of the Fathers set out, with the whole of the· boys belonging to the College, for a long excursion, and on these occasions are accompanied by the College band which does great credit to the musical instruction imparted by the professors. No prettier sight did we witness at Einsiedeln than when, on the sound of music being heard in the distance, every one hastened to the windows to see the great gates of the College thrown open, and the long procession of boys in their soutanes, and of the Fathers in their habits, issuing forth, and setting out merrily on the road.

Our stay at Einsiedeln was marked by one tragical occurrence, namely, the death by drowning of two of the best and most promising youths in the College. They were both of them out-boarders, and had been accustomed to go several times a week to bathe in the Sihl, which in many places is a very dangerous river, on account of the deep holes occurring in its bed. However, as several accidents had already happened there before, a safe bathing place had been constructed for the boys, but on this sad evening one of the two youths already mentioned, passed for some reason or other, beyond the bounds of safety. His companion, seeing that he was sinking, hastened to him in the hopes of saving him. But his efforts were of no avail, and both boys were drowned. Their bodies were not recovered till the following day, when they were placed in coffins and carried to the Chapel attached to the School, whence the funeral took place the following morning and was most impressive. All the Fathers, all the College boys, and most of the inhabitants of the village, in a long and mournful procession, followed the bier, on which were placed, side by side, the two coffins completely hidden beneath masses of roses, lilies and other bright, sweet-scented, summer flowers. For some time, every evening at seven o' clock, all the out-door pupils assembled at the foot of the great crucifix placed at the head of the road leading to the cemetery, and then, preceded by one of the Fathers, walked slowly along saying their rosaries. As soon as they had reached the graves, each of which had a Cross at its head with a white crape veil over it, the graves themselves being covered with flowers, the Father recited the prayers for the dead, after. which they all returned quietly and in silence to the place whence they had set out, not surely without having received an impressive lesson, calculated to profit them during the whole of their after lives.

The cemetery at Einsiedeln is about a quarter of a mile from the village, and is beautifully situated at the foot of the green and wooded heights which rise to the South of the Monastery. When we were there it looked lovely, every grave being planted with the same kind of flowers, pinks and white saxifrage. Unlike many cemeteries in other parts of Switzerland, it is affectionately cared for, and it is clear that the honour due to the dear remains of their dead is a duty

which is religiously performed by the inhabitants
of Einsiedeln.

In common with the Convent Church, the cemetery is never empty. Every evening numbers may
be seen wending their way thither, their prayer-
books in their hands, and saying their rosaries,
and as long as man or boy remains within its
precincts he keeps his head uncovered, taking off
his hat even if only passing it hastily. Along
the walls are placed the Stations of the Cross,
it being considered better to have them there
than in the Church, because such persons as
repair to the cemetery to make them can hardly
help saying, at the same time, a prayer for the
dead who are resting around them. The children's
graves, as in most Swiss cemeteries, occupy a
place set apart. On nearly all of these tiny
mounds are placed bright green mosses generally in the form of a cross, or they are surmounted by little marble crucifixes and monuments of equally small dimensions. I know no
more affecting sight than that of these little
graves, set close to one another, with their touching memorials testifying the faith and hope, the
love and sorrow of the parents. The mortality
among children is very great at Einsiedeln, but
when the period of infancy is safely passed, the
inhabitants generally attain to a good old age.

In the centre of the cemetery is a large cross, to which is affixed, not the whole body of Our Lord, but only His Face on the Handkerchief of Veronica, His Hands, and His Feet. The Chapel is commodious and simple in its structure. Adjoining to it is a Bone-house where rows of skulls, with the name and date of the death painted on the forehead, are ranged upon shelves. Strange though it may seem, it is nevertheless true, that not many years ago, when the cemetery was re-opened, as it is called, that is to say when the old graves are once more used, it was not an uncommon practice for survivors of deceased relatives to take possession of their skulls and keep them in their own houses. A lady at Einsiedeln told me that she quite well remembered seeing, in the bed chamber of a friend, the skulls of her father and mother, placed under a glass-case.

The inhabitants of Einsiedeln seem to me a population such as is now-a-days but seldom to be met with in other parts of Switzerland and especially in such portions as are the resort of tourists. The same impression was made upon the Viscomte de Melun when he visited Einsiedeln. „It was not only the glaciers and the Monastery“, he says in his „Souvenir“, which I admired, but also everything which piety had added to the

creation in order to speak of God to man. Each
of the mountains has its chapel, its patronage,
and its pilgrimage, while at intervals the Stations
of the Cross call for a prayer and pious thoughts;
the stranger moreover is saluted with the sweet
greeting „Blessed be Jesus Christ", and when wea-
ried and wanting repose he may always find a seat
placed before a Cross or a holy picture, or else
a little Chapel open for rest as well as devotion.
Catholicism is here the *principle* as well as the
foundation of everything, it does not merely
form a portion of a thousand other interests,
men remain always in the presence of God,
and the Cross surmounts their Town-house as
well as their churches."

The character of the inhabitants is genial,
self-respecting and industrious, thrifty, but free
from the grasping, greedy spirit which charac-
terises many of their fellow countrymen; well
educated and liberal minded, they set a bright
example, not only to their own nation, but to all
who come in contact with them. Grounded in the
doctrines and practices of their religion from their
childhood upwards they are, for the most part,
profoundly pious, and, as I said before, there
is hardly a man, woman, or child in Einsiedeln
who does not assist at one or other of the daily
Masses, unless prevented by duty or illness.

At Einsiedeln, for the first time, since I had left Rome I witnessed the beautiful and affecting sight of a Priest carrying the Blessed Sacrament to a sick person, preceded by a boy ringing a bell and carrying a lighted lamp. There also, as in the Eternal City, every one knelt on the ground in reverence and adoration while Our Lord passed by. Another day the Curé in his cotta went on horseback to some distant village, bearing the Blessed Sacrament, and, as before, the people knelt in the road and in front of their houses, as soon as the tinkling of the bell announced the approach of Our Lord.

All the time that I was at Einsiedeln I never saw any one drunk in the street, a striking contrast to what I had been accustomed to in the Canton Vaud, and cases of immorality, I am told, are equally rare in the district; truly the spirit of virtue that prevails at Einsiedeln is an important ingredient in the charm of a sojourn there. A French lady whom I met at our Hotel assured me that, after visiting all the principal shrines in France and Italy she awarded the palm to Einsiedeln, because of the spirit of piety which prevails among its people.

In common with the other „Little Cantons", as the „Forest Cantons" of Switzerland are called, Schwytz has been always governed in a peaceable

manner, none of the difficulties with which some
of the other Cantons have to contend having
ever occurred in its administration.

Just opposite our windows was a kind of
village green, at the further end of which stands
the School, a very large, commodious building,
as indeed it needs to be to hold upwards of
seven hundred children. The boys and girls
attend in almost equal numbers, I do not know
how many masters are employed, but the girls
have seven mistresses assisted by a goodly
number of pupil-teachers. At intervals between
their various lessons the children have a quarter
of an hours recreation, and at such times it was
curious to see the girls playing at our old English
games of *oranges and lemons, threading the needle,
hunt the slipper* and *Blind man's buff;* as for the
boys their principal amusement seemed to consist in running after one another, until the one
who was caught, being thrown on the ground by
his captor, was soundly flogged, the punishment
being received by the victim with unvarying
patience and good humour. If, in the midst of
their games, any of them chanced to perceive the
Curé, or one of the Fathers passing along the
road, there was a general rush of girls and boys
towards him, each anxious to obtain the smile,
or kind word, or shake of the hand which the

good Fathers seem never weary of bestowing. Once or twice in the week the boys are drilled, and it was most amusing to watch the awkward squad of little fellows going through their exercises and marching along, the majority of them with naked feet.

During the summer time the children seldom wear shoes and stockings, however well to do their parents may be, excepting of course on Sundays and Feast-days, when both boys and girls are always dressed in their best.

Every day they have a Mass said for them in the School Chapel, and on the Sundays they have their own high Mass and very often a procession. It is pretty to see it passing round the green, the very little children dressed in white, as well as some of the elder girls, and the Curé at their head. As soon as it has re-entered the School-chapel the great procession issues from the Monastery Church. On high festivals, the Abbot takes part in it, carrying a statue of the Blessed Virgin, and accompanied by the whole of the Fathers all the pupils of the College and numbers of the Parishioners. Three splendid banners are borne by sacristans whilst others carry on a platform an immense statue of Our Blessed Lady. Marshalled in due order the procession descends the great steps and, after having made the circuit of the Place, re-enters the Church when High Mass immediately begins. During the College vacations the absence of the long stream of boys in their white cottas and soutanes makes a great void in the procession, and the sweet harmony of their young voices is much missed in the church-music.

But a portion of the boys who belong to the choir return to their posts after an absence of a week only, and spend the remainder of their holidays at the Monastery taking long excursions with the Fathers, or amusing themselves with acting plays in the College-theatre. We happened to be at Einsiedeln when the summer vacation commenced. The Sunday before breaking up all the boys assembled in the Court below the Abbot's apartments and gave a vocal and instrumental concert. All the windows on that side of the Monastery were thrown wide open and at them were gathered the Fathers, in whose honour the performance was given, while the whole of the vacant space was crowded by a delighted audience. The song with which the concert concluded is centuries old, and it is only lately that the music and words have been printed; it has fifteen verses, of which the following will serve as a specimen.

A, A, A, Valete studia,
Omnia jam tædia
Vertuntur in gaudia,
A, A, A, Valete studia.

E, E, E, Ite miseriæ,
  Ite, ite lacrymæ
  Læti sumus hodie;
E, E, E, Ite miseriæ!

I, I, I, Vale professor mi!
  Valeas ad optimum,
  Cures me ad minimum.
I, I, I, Vale professor mi!

O, O, O, Magno cum gaudio
  Einsidlam relinquimus,
  Patriam repetimus.
O, O, O, Magno cum gaudio.

U, U, U, Læto cum spiritu
  Libros nunc abjicimus,
  Poculum accipimus. '
U, U, U, Læto cum spiritu.

The remaining verses are in German, the tune,
a very lively one, rang in our ears for long
afterwards. Then the boys, amidst much applause,
set off on a march round the precincts of the
Monastery, still singing to the accompaniment of
their band their *A, A, A, valete &c.* On nearing
the cemetery, the merry voices were hushed into
silence, and the boys gathering round the graves
of their dead comrades, chanted the Litany of
the Blessed Virgin and the „De Profundis", after
which they all of them returned silently, and
quietly, to the Monastery. The following morning
High Mass was celebrated with a full orchestre

and all the boys received Holy Communion. In an hour or two afterwards they were starting for their various destinations, only, before leaving the College, they went, some singly, some in parties of half a dozen, to say a prayer before the Holy Chapel. It was a very edifying scene the seriousness and recollection of the boys being most delightful to witness.

There are many charming walks in the neighbourhood of Einsiedeln, though in the heat of summer there is a great want of shade in the vicinity of the Monastery. Suggestions have often been made to the Fathers respecting the advantages of planting trees, so as to form avenues along the neighbouring roads, but the Monks preferred to lay out a most attractive walk, leading from the Monastery up the hills. There, in the woods which cover the sides of all the neighbouring heights, a pleasant shade can always be found, and in the early mornings, or evenings, nothing can be more delightful than the rambles along the different vallies branching out from Einsiedeln. On every road and field path are placed at intervals way-side Chapels with quaint ornaments and pictures, offering to the pedestrian at once a place of devotion and shelter from the heat. Pillars are also often to be seen, supporting a framework on which is placed a picture of

Our Lord, and I seldom saw the peasants pass them without taking off their hats or kneeling down to say a prayer. In the village itself, at the foot of the principal street, is an immense crucifix before which lights are kept burning during the night. In fact wherever the eyes turn they rest upon some sacred object calculated to lift the soul to Heaven.

It is of course to be expected that at the height at which Einsiedeln is situated above the sea the winters should be severe. They are not, however exceptionally so. Even in the coldest months of the year pilgrimages are continually made to the Shrine of Our Lady of the Hermits, though not in such great numbers as in the summer. Throughout the winter the Church is well frequented even at the early Masses which, as in summer, begin at four o' clock. On the Feast of St. Meinrad, which occurs in January, multitudes visit his Chapel on the Etzel, together with the Benedictine Fathers who go there in sledges, accompanied by all the boys of the College.

Of the kind of weather prevailing during the year a good idea may be gained from a note book kept by one of the officials connected with the Monastery. We find from it that on the 19th of January 1724 snow fell incessantly and was already knee deep. Traces of two wolves had, moreover, been seen. The 21st of January was the festival of St. Meinrad, but there was so much wind and snow that no one could venture out of doors. On the 15th February the chronicler mentions that an old cart driver in the service of the community, aged 78, donned a masquerade dress and went thro' a performance to the astonishment of all the beholders. During the months of February and March the weather was beautiful and not cold, but there was often snow and fog. The 11th April (Cœna Domini) was fine, then came snow and rain again. In May there were „beautiful dews" and lovely days. In June there fell a good deal of rain and there was but little sun. July, August and September were lovely months. In October also, the weather was splendid. On the 30th of December, the roads were in good order for sledging and up to the 31st the weather remained beautiful and mild, though at intervals snow had fallen.

A favourite excursion during winter is to a beautiful Alpine village called Yberg. Of an annual pilgrimage made there by the Benedictine Fathers, Fr Gall Morel has given a charming idyllic picture, in a poem of which the following extracts, roughly „overset" into English, may enable the reader to form some idea.

THE PILGRIMAGE TO YBERG.

Dawn flushed all the sky, and pale grew the stars
    in the heavens.
Sweetly sounded the bells of Einsiedeln's beautiful
    cloister.
The people in crowds and with prayers followed the
    fluttering banners,
Slowly borne down the aisles and out thro' the wide
    open portals,
While resounded the chants sung in honour of Mary
    Our Mother.
And I with my brethren, clothed in choir habits care-
    fully plaited,
Joined with delight in the songs of the pious suppliant
    people.
The annual pilgrimage making to the mountainous village
    of Yberg;
A pilgrimage dating from out the dim and far distant
    ages,
When the hapless Chevalier Amberg, his soul overwhelmed
    with anguish,
Decreed that for him and his son pious prayers should
    yearly be offered.
And so we went on our way, in the pleasant cool of the
    morning,
Through the vale which the swift flowing Sihl in its
    many meanderings waters.
Melodiously mingled the tinkle of bells with the sound
    of our chanting;
And the loud jödlings of herdsmen from the velvety
    grass-covered uplands,
Whilst up in the ether the larks, soaring high, were
    exultingly singing.

Descr. of Einsiedeln.   12

Little by little the valley grew narrow and Alpine giants
        high towering,
Enclosed it well nigh within a steadfast immoveable
        circle,
Awe-inspiring their snow-peaks rise high into the beau-
        tiful azure.
Already the sun had ascended above their lofty far away
        summits,
And its beams were lighting and warming the valley of
        peace and seclusion,
When suddenly down from a lovely and verdant slope
        of the mountain
Yberg's Church looked smiling upon us, encircled by
        numerous chalets.
Brightly shone the dear House of the Lord midst its som-
        bre and lowly surroundings,
And there also stood the good Priest, full of zeal in the
        midst of his people,
Looking up to the God of all mercy as he prayed for
        the flock of His pasture,
E'en as the tower soars above the chalets gathered
        around it.
Singing, we drew nearer and nearer to the Alp circled
        village of Yberg,
Which born at the foot of the mountains, in deepest
        retirement and quiet,
Rests like an infant asleep on the calm loving breast of
        its Mother.
Joyous and fearless and strong, as healthy in soul as in
        body,
Are the peasants who dwell there, true Switzers of
        happy and pastaway ages,
Even such as we see them depicted in old-world legends
        and stories,

Or in pious heart stirring songs flowing forth from the
soul of the poet.
Then as we approached to our goal, preceded by fluttering
banners,
A welcome to give us, advanced the worthy Priest of
the village.
And up to the temple of old to God dedicated he
led us,
To share in the feast instituted by Jesus Our. Lord and
Our Saviour,
Ere His children He left and to God His Father in
Heaven ascended.
That His own upon Him might think, with holy love
overflowing.
Ah! that feast which to thousands brings strength and
comfort and healing,
To the living and also the dead in the dreary realms of
flames purifying,
Whom we pray for, clad as to day, in sombre habits of
mourning,
Deeply bewailing the fate of our fellows reduced into
dust and to ashes,
Whilst the knell of the deep sounding bell resounds thro'
the aisles of the temple.

.   .   .   .

.   .   .   . And now the Sacrifice ended
Many in quiet are praying, and many canticles singing,
E'en as the peasants are wont to raise up their voices
to Heaven.
Then to a different repast we were, one and all of us,
summoned,
A repast which to the body might give its needful refreshment.

Ere this the glorious sun had already the height of the
heavens
Almost ascended, when called by the kindly voice of
the pastor,
My brethren and I round the well-spread table were
gathered.
The pleasant time of refreshment with affectionate converse being shortened,
Longing to wander away in the verdant, velvety pastures,
To all who were present at table I said: let us
ramble
Up to the surging torrent which hastes raging out of
the Thalgrund,
Guggern the name it is known by, that into its dread-
ful abysses
Our eyes may gaze awe inspired. All applauded my
words and consented;
Many rose up at once, only a few of the weary and
aged,
Or of those retained by their glass, remaining seated at
table.
Many, too, of the women, the boys and the peasants
came with us,
Also the worthy shepherd of souls accompanied with
gladness his people.
Up through the meads clad in verdure, and by pathways
softly ascending,
Need I describe all the pleasure of such friendly heart-
cheering rambles,
Or tell of the fragrance cast forth by ambrosian Alpine
sprung flowrets
Or of the heart lightening, dark blue, mountainous
ether,

Or of the sound of the cow-bells tinkling from far and
　　　　　around us,
Or of the tones of the horns re-echoing into the
　　　　　valley?
These things thou knowest thyself and like me thou
　　　　　hast often enjoyed them.

.　.　.　.　.　.　.　.　.　.　.　.　.　.　.

Scarcely half of the way o'er lofty rocks had we clam-
　　　　　bered,
When suddenly stretched out before us a lovely grass-
　　　　　covered upland,
Tempting our footsteps to stay and gaze on the beauti-
　　　　　ful prospect.
Astonished the eye swept over the snowy peaks of the
　　　　　mountains,
To the left and the right and around us, a temple to
　　　　　God consecrated.
There by many a lake and many a ravine and
　　　　　valley,
Dwell in quiet and peace and joy the noble race of the
　　　　　Schwytzers.

.　.　.　.　.　.　.　.　.　.　.　.　.　.　.

Low alpine shrubs grew all round the flower and grass-
　　　　　covered upland,
Where berries of sweetness and fragrance are eagerly
　　　　　sought for by children.
Traces of walls built in ages gone by showed here and
　　　　　there through the bushes.
Resting upon the green sward we gazed delightedly
　　　　　round us.
The little lambs skipped at our feet, and goats leaped
　　　　　from one rock to another,
Well watched by the eyes of a boy lying down in the
　　　　　midst of the pasture,

His rustic pipe playing, then singing a jubilant song of
the mountains,
Which as he saw us draw near, he broke off and suddenly ended.

. . . .

Then the good Shepherd of Souls addressing himself to
the cowherd,
Come hither my boy, he exclaimed, sit down, and bring
your pipe with you,
And sing to our friends the song of the Castle whose
ruins are round us.
Then he got up, but slowly and as though he were almost unwilling.
Nathless feeling he must, for so his good Pastor had
willed it.
Shyly nearer he drew, then seated himself on the
ruins,
Whilst all of us gathered around him to list to his tale
of the foretime.
First from his pipe he drew forth a strain of sorrowful
music,
Such as the wanderer oft hears the shepherds play on
the mountain,
Making the heart of the listener overflow with a sweet
and a yearning sadness.
Then with clear voice he began to sing the sorrowful
legend of Yberg.

telling how a maiden with pale face and sad
countenance stood in days gone by in the moon-
light before a lordly castle, whilst a wild north-
wind chased the clouds across the sky. Ravens
croaked around her as she uttered her com-

plaint, exclaiming: „And is it thus that thou hast forsaken me, thou faithless, Knight? Ah me! Ah me! full well I know that what thou hast done to me God will certainly avenge. For He is the Strength of the weak, He sets down the deeds of the wicked and punishes their infamy."

Whilst the maiden was thus making her complaint there issued forth, like a mocking echo, from out the chambers of the castle, sounds of mirth and jollity. In the great hall, intoxicated with pleasure, sat the young Knight von Amberg, and to the sound of the zither indulged in rude riot with his friends. The maiden, seized with shuddering horror, tottered to the edge of the precipice on which the castle stood and gazed into the abyss, as though unknowing and unconscious of what she did. She is about to fall into it, when suddenly she beholds, standing by her side her two brothers, who, seizing hold of her, cry out, „Sister what art thou doing here?" She looks fixedly and long at both the well-known faces, and then exclaims as though distraught with grief, „Oh false, false Knight!" But the brothers hold their peace, and return in silence to their dwelling, leading their sister with them. Then having placed her there in safety they hasten forth, bent on taking their revenge.

Now the old Knight von Amberg filled the

office of judge at that time in the Canton of
Schwytz, and so it was to him that the brothers
brought their plaint. But the two avengers did
not divulge the name of the criminal to the judge,
who carefully examined into the evidence laid
before him. The next morning he summoned
them again to appear at the judgment seat. Then
raising his voice in the presence of all the people
he cried out: „Alas! for what has chanced upon
our Alpine heights! Wo to him by whom the
evil deed was done! Wo to him by whom the
maiden's honour was so shamefully destroyed;
even though he were my son it should avail him
nothing; he shall die by the sword, be he knight
or be he peasant, who in secret decoyed a
pure maiden and robbed her of her fair fame.
Accusers take my knightly sword, and in accordance with your rights bring the craven wretch
before me. Obediently they departed and quickly
returned with von Amberg's only son, in order
that his father might take vengeance upon him
for the crime he had committed.

As when in a storm the thunderbolt falls, so
the grey-headed old man sank to the ground.
Then looking upon his son, he exclaimed in his
agony „Oh God, oh God, is it indeed too late?
Ah me the sentence has been pronounced, and
the deed has gone before the Majesty of the

Almighty!" Then the broken hearted Father
withdrew to his chamber, whilst like a plaint there
mingled with his grief the knell of the funeral
bell. To Heaven he turned his stony gaze and
wrung his trembling hands „Oh God of Heaven,"
he cried, „have mercy on my child's soul." Laying
down his office he left his castle and sought a
home on Yberg's rocks. There he built for
himself a dwelling and passed his time in prayer,
until the lamp of his life was extinguished by
death.

The sorrowful story ended, for a space we were all
of us speechless.
Thinking over in silence the gone by, terrible
sorrow,
Yet living e'en now in song as vivid as in the a-
fore time.
Whilst many wiped away tears which coursed slowly
down from their eyelids.
But when the Pastor perceived it, the worthy Priest of
his people,
Speaking in soft sounding tones he exclaimed, it seemeth
unto me,
Almost as if the sad song of the lad our innocent pleasure had troubled.
So let us cease for a while to speak of the tragical
story,
And bend our steps towards home for the sun to the
westward is hastening.
Neither is time remaining to scale the heights rising
around us,

That we may thence gaze awe stricken into the depths
of the Thalgrund.
But we have looked far down into lifes still more fearful abysses,
Which cannot be sounded by lead or by our own un-
derstanding.
He spoke, and quickly we hastened home to the house
of the Pastor.
Then in the low rustic chamber of the friendly and
pastoral chalet
We gathered together once more. Too soon came the
hour of departure,
But where is the Pastor? Ah see! even now he makes
his appearance,
In his right hand bearing a cross, a black one painted
all over,
And in his left holding a skull, ghastly, and grinning,
and fearful.
Astonished we all gazed upon him with looks of long-
ing enquiry.
Till at last spoke in these words the worthy Pastor of
Yberg.
»Moved by the tragical story of the fate of the Ritter
von Amberg,
Look on these sorrowful relics, thro' centuries carefully
guarded;
Gaze on the sign of all comfort that of old the grave
overshadowed,
Where, resting from sorrow and pain, the Knight lay
mid peasants and shepherds;
Look on the skull where first dwelt his noble and chi-
valrous spirit,
See the holes whence the eyes looked so boldly with
angry flashes like lightning,

When injustic or crime were but named, or else unmasked
in his presence;
But which lovingly smiled on the good; glistening with
pleasure and gladness.
Look at the sternly set mouth which once penance or
freedom awarded,
Or with heaviest sorrow o'erwhelmed, bewailed his son,
his beloved.
Dumb and blind and unconscious are now the remains,
which aforetime
And once — but foolish and hard and far from fit-
ting
Is what I have spoken to men who are better and wiser
than I am.»
Thus saying he hasted forthwith to the room, where in
silence and quiet,
The cross and the skull lie at rest, the one by the side
of the other.
Then rising we went to the Church, and gathered in
front of the altar, ‹
Praying in stillness and silence awhile, to God our Father
and Leader,
To the dear Saviour of all, and to the holy Mother of
sorrows,
Laying with trust in their hands our past and present
and future.
But now see the sun hastens on to sink 'neath the snow
covered mountains,
While smilingly fall his last beams on the kneeling
crowd in the chapel;
E'en as they fall on the altar, gracious sign of a merciful
answer.
So then after pressing the hand of the worthy Pastor
of Yberg,

Bidding him hearty farewell, I quitted the pastoral
valley,
Wending my way back to the hearth of my Lares and
well loved Penates.

Some time ago a quarrel arose between the
village of Yberg and an adjacent one respecting
the site that was to be chosen for a Church
which was intended to serve both villages. The
result was a happier one than often attends such
altercations. The conclusion ultimately arrived
at was to build a Church and also a School-
house in each village. A friend of mine, who
went to Yberg just after the building of the
Church had begun, on the occasion of the
festival of the patron saint of the village, which
occurs in mid-winter, told me that it was a most
touching and interesting sight to see the peasants
driving up to the village from their far-away
dwellings on the mountain, each bringing with
him, on his sledge, a large stone as his contri-
bution to the erection of the sacred edifice.

Something has been already said in the account given at the commencement of this little
book of the Hotels of Einsiedeln, and I can certainly add my testimony to the good food and
comfortable rooms to be found therein. A German author who, not long ago, published an
account of his travels in France remarks that

all sorts and conditions of men are to be found among the Saints, with the single exception of Hotel Keepers, which shows how very difficult it must be for such people to save their souls. I think, however, that amongst the hosts of the guest-houses at Einsiedeln, the majority may be considered as not belonging to the category on which the learned Doctor passes so sweeping a censure.

The Salle à manger of our hotel resembled the refectory of a Monastery rather than the dining room of an inn, a large crucifix hanging on its walls and opposite it a beautiful picture of Blessed Nicholas of Flüe by Deschwanden.

Our great object of interest during our stay at the Hotel du Paon was the visitor's book, which contains hundreds of distinguished names of pilgrims, most of whom come only for a day and then depart; at the table d'hôte there is a constant succession of fresh faces of people from all quarters of the globe, the party one day including a Japanese. All kinds of Religious Orders may also be seen there, both Nuns and Monks, and the number of different languages spoken is legion.

I have already alluded to the high state of civilisation of the inhabitants of Einsiedeln. This is to be attributed, in a large measure, to the in-

fluence of the Benedictine Fathers, who are, of
course, the great benefactors of the district. The
condition of the roads, the appearance of the
fields, the well built, well cared-for cottages on the
property belonging to the Monastery, all testify
to the excellence of their administration, and the
good example given by them to the farmers and
peasants far and near. The Monastery is celebrated for its breed of horses, and must have been
equally famous at one time for its breed of cows,
seeing that in the year 1748, the King of Poland
sent one of his herdsmen thither to purchase
some of the monastery cows, similar to those
which he had bought twenty years before.

Next to the Convent, the extensive commercial
pursuits of Messrs Benziger exercise the most beneficial influence in keeping permanently employed
about 700 hands. The whole village follows the
brilliant example set by this enterprising firm.
This is proved by the fact that loungers are
never seen in the village, here everybody works.

Messrs Benziger have established, among other
philanthropical institutions, a house for their young
apprentices, some forty in number, who are placed
under the care of three Sisters of Charity. Early
in the morning and at bed-time we often used
to hear the tinkling of the bell summoning the
youths to prayer.

The Square facing the Monastery.

As I have already mentioned in chapter VIII,
a visit to the establishments of Messrs Charles and
Nicholas Benziger Brothers is also one of the great
interests of Einsiedeln which no one will undertake
without deriving much pleasure and instruction.

It is scarcely possible to think of the artistical
productions of the above firm without re-
membering the name of M. P. von Deschwanden
who worked so much for it. This great Swiss
artist, whose recent death has been so deeply
regretted, used to take special delight to be employed for poor Churches, and indeed he did not
care to use his brush unless his productions were
to be devoted to religious purposes. A native
of Stans, and of good family, the cultivated,
pious, kindly man was beloved and esteemed
by all who came in contact with him, whilst his
modesty was so great that he never alluded to
his works in any way. One of the Fathers, Rev.
Dr Kuhn, has recently written his life, which will,
doubtless, be as interesting as that of Father
Gall Morel published a few years ago. Theodore
Deschwanden, a younger brother, who died at the
early age of 22, seems to have been possessed
of equal, if not greater genius than Paul, if we
may judge from his picture of the death of
the Blessed Virgin, which is in the Chapel of
the orphanage on the heights opposite Einsiedeln.

He died before it was finished and the last touches were put in by his elder brother.

Although miracles are constantly being wrought at Einsiedeln, the Fathers do not approve of publicity being given to them, on account of the times in which we live. Unbelievers, they say, would but scoff at them, and good Catholics do not need to hear of them. Some few, however, which have occurred are so interesting that I cannot refrain from given an account of them.

Going back to the last century, we find that on the 8th of September 1748, the Archbishop of Vienna preached a sermon in honour of Our Lady, and in his exordium spoke of the miracle worked on himself at Vienna the year before, when he was lying ill of a dangerous malady. On the vigil of the Nativity of the Blessed Virgin he had been given up by three Doctors, after every remedy had been tried without avail. Death was quickly approaching, when he made a vow that if it should please God to restore him to health he would go on a pilgrimage to Einsiedeln, and, to the astonishment of all, the following day, and without taking any medicine, he was perfectly well. The Doctors on visiting him were surprised to find him alive. His sermon, we are told, was so touching that it made tears flow from many eyes.

The other cases which I shall mention have
occurred in more recent years. The first is that
of a servant of the Count de M. at Innspruck
who, after living thirty years in his family, became,
by degrees, entirely blind. She had been so faithful a domestic, that she was not allowed to leave
her master's house. Chancing to hear, from one
of the members of the household, of the miracles
wrought at Einsiedeln she was seized with a
longing to go here, but was told, over and over
again, that, utterly blind as she was, it would be
impossible for her to undertake the long and
arduous journey. At last, however, moved by
her entreaties, her master arranged that a fellow
servant should accompany her to the shrine.
They set off on foot on the 14th of August, and
reached Einsiedeln on the 7th of September.
Arrived there, the two women hastened to the
Church, where she who was blind prayed most
earnestly to Our Lady of the Hermits that her
sight might be restored. But, at the conclusion
of the Novena which she began that day, she
was as blind as ever, and with a half broken
heart prepared to set off on her journey back
to Innspruck. Before doing so, however, she
went to bid the friend from whom I heard
the story, goodbye, „Ah Mademoiselle" she exclaimed „you see it has not pleased the Blessed

Virgin to cure me." Then she went back to the
Church to say a farewell prayer, rose from her
knees and on reaching the door cried out to her
companion „Why! what has happened to me —
I see houses, trees, people, I see your black
dress and your white cap!" Then she began to
laugh and to cry, and almost running back
to the Holy Chapel, prostrated herself on the
pavement, and remained there for a long space
of time offering up with sobs and tears her
thanks to God. From that time she made a
pilgrimage on foot every year to Einsiedeln, the
basket which she carried on her back being always
laden with tapers for the shrine of Our Blessed
Lady. It was the Count de M., her master, who
as a thank-offering for the miracle wrought upon
his servant, erected in one of the side-chapels
in the Monastery Church the beautiful altar of
the Sacred Heart.

The second miracle of which I heard was
performed in favour of a Sister of Charity who,
whilst still a Novice, became blind of both eyes.
It was arranged that an operation should be
performed by a physician at Lucerne, on a certain
Monday morning. The previous Saturday the
young Novice went to Einsiedeln, not, as she
said, to ask Our Lady to cure her, but to obtain
through her all-powerful intercession, fortitude to

bear the operation. The night on which she reached her destination she had intense pain in her eyes, and the next morning, when about to receive Holy Communion, it became so intolerable that she could hardly endure it. Just as the Priest put the Host on her tongue the agony was so great that involuntarily she put her hand to her eyes and when she took it away found that she could see as well and clearly as ever she had done in her life.

A third miracle, and one of a very remarkable kind, was wrought on a young girl belonging to the Department of Doubs in France who, while quite a child, had received such injuries as to render her a perfect cripple. Her arms were bent at the elbow and her hands nailed as it were to her shoulders; she could neither feed herself nor move, for her legs were bent in the same way as her hands. She had been to the first physicians in Paris, but they all pronounced her case hopeless, and added that nothing could be done to alleviate her sufferings. At last her relatives resolved to take her to Einsiedeln, and on arriving there she was wheeled in her little cart into the Church, just as Mass was being celebrated at the High altar. At the Elevation a noise was heard which startled the congregation, most of whom imagined that something had

fallen from the roof. But the persons who chanced to be standing near the little cart were aware
that the sound proceeded from the girl suddenly
rising, standing upright in her cart, then stepp-
ing out of it, and prostrating herself before the
holy statue, at the same time crying out „I am
cured, I am cured!" A telegram was instantly
despatched to the Curé of her parish, but at first
the people there would not credit the news.
The girl remained at Einsiedeln till the gover-
ment officials at Schwytz and the Abbot had
caused enquiry to be made into all the circum-
stances attendant upon the miracle, and had veri-
fied the certficates of the French physicians. When
at last she returned home, all the people of her
own parish, and of the villages situated far and
wide, went out to meet her in procession, and a
splendid robe of cloth of gold, the same in which
the statue of Our Lady has ever since been
vested on the festival of the 14ᵗʰ September was
sent by them as a votive offering to Einsiedeln.

Another miracle of which I heard was wrought
upon a blind girl whose parents lived at Besançon.
One of their children, a youth of 12, had been
sent to the College at Einsiedeln and hearing
of the miracles which were constantly occurring
he wrote to his father, begging him to bring his
sister there. Accordingly, soon after, the whole

family set out on foot on their pilgrimage to the
shrine. The girl was cured and the father made
a vow to pay an annual pilgrimage to Einsiedeln.
Since his death the son who was educated there,
and is now a Priest, has taken his father's vow
upon himself, and whilst we were at Einsiedeln
he made his annual pilgrimage to Our Lady of
the Hermits.

In his „Souvenir de voyage“ the Count de
Melun states that his Mother had been seized
with a sudden and dangerous illness the previous
winter, and that very soon she was given up by
the Doctors. Already her family were gathered
round her bed, weeping and imagining they were
listening to her last words, when suddenly the
remembrance of Our Lady of the Hermits, whose
shrine the Viscount had recently visited, flashed
upon his recollection like a ray of hope. Hastening to a neighbouring Church he made a vow
that, if his Mother were spared, he would make
a Pilgrimage to Einsiedeln to thank Our Lady
for her cure. Very soon afterwards the Doctor
was able to conquer the malady and the invalid
was restored to perfect health.

Wonderful, however, as are the corporeal miracles performed at Einsiedeln of those a spiritual
kind are still more so. The numbers of conver-
sions which are constantly taking place there, and

the abundance of graces vouchsafed in answer to prayer are fully known to God alone, though in part they are also known to the good Fathers into whose ears are daily poured the secrets of overburdened, erring, contrite souls.

At last came the day of our departure from Einsiedeln. A last visit to the Holy Chapel, a last look at the Church and the Monastery and we had bidden farewell, probably for ever, to the Sanctuary in the „dark wood" where we had spent so many happy days, the recollection of which will ever fill a treasured place in our memories. If pilgrimages had no other use than that of removing us for a time out of every-day life, and lifting the soul from the dust that it may ascend on the wings of prayer to heaven in spots peculiarly sanctified by God they would need no further justification. And if there be any place on earth in which everything around one tends to raise the heart to God, it surely is Einsiedeln. Of it may with truth he said

> Omnia si lustres alienæ
> Climata terræ,
> Non est in toto sanctior
> Orbe locus.

F^r GALL MOREL'S POEMS

TRANSLATED FROM THE GERMAN.

The Pilgrim's Prayer.

THERE, where in an Alpine vale
High the Holy Chapel stands,
And where with rejoicing songs
Journey many pilgrim bands.
Draw me also, Mary mild,
To adore Thee and thy Child!
Mary mild,
Star in desert drear and wild.

There, where crowds have comfort found,
There, where wounds have all been healed,
Where St. Meinrad shed his blood,
And where Saints their faith have sealed,
Draw me also, Mary mild,
To adore Thee and thy Child!
Mary mild,
Star in darkness drear and wild.

Where the burden of its sin
Falls from off the o'er laden heart,
And inspired with trust the child
From his mother cannot part.

Draw me also, Mary mild,
To adore Thee and thy Child!
Mary mild,
Star in desert drear and wild.

Where before the sacred shrine,
Bitter tears have oft been shed,
Many souls been reconciled,
Many wanderers to thee led,
Draw me also, Mary mild,
To adore Thee and thy Child!
Mary mild,
Star in desert drear and wild.

There may I, too, weep and pray,
And before Thee bowing down.
Weave, oh Mother pure and sweet,
Rosary garlands for thy crown;
Thither draw me, Mary mild,
To adore Thee and thy Child!
Mary mild,
Star in desert drear and wild.

Mother, full of mercy, hear,
Turn thy children not away,
Show to us thy own dear Son,
Hear thy suppliants while they pray
And draw near Thee, Mary mild,
To adore Thee and thy Child!
Mary mild,
Star in desert drear and wild.

The Pilgrim's arrival.

Ah! what fresh marvel is it that he sees!
And who has this majestic temple built,
Which like a mountain rises up to heaven,
And thence in royal guise on him looks down?
Who was it that conceived this splendid fane,
Before whose majesty his soul is awed?
Who was it that upreared these vaulted doors
Thro' whose wide cavities the people throng?

Now from the Minster towers he hears resound,
Throughout the air, loud heart-inspiring tones;
From every height and through the vale advance
The Pilgrim folk, with swift and eager step,
Their staffs in hand and wallets on their back;
And never empty is the village street.
For aye, new bands of pilgrims issue forth
And with their crowds afresh the valley fill.

From far and near the noble nations come,
From ancient Rhine and from the shores of Aar,
From all the beauteous provinces of France,
From snowy mountains and from lowly vales,
Where dwell the free-born sons of Switzerland;
From Swabia and far off German realms,
From many a distant spot they hither stream;
From the warm South and from the chilly North.

The Pilgrim's entrance into the Church.

What feelings born of joy o'ercome him here!
Unutterable! never felt before.
How pants his heart with quick redoubled pulse!
How swells his inmost breast with lofty thoughts!

And now his eyes are filled with happy tears.
He rises high above the desert world,
And longs to sing of all his spirit feels.
But ah! his tongue is impotent and dumb.

He sees how midst majestic columns placed,
A dome within a dome the Chapel stands!
And how, midst many golden lightning rays
The Virgin is enshrined in majesty.
He sees the nations how they haste within,
And sees how brightly burns devotion's flame.
He comes, beholds, and humbly bows him down,
His soul with sweet emotions overawed.

Then on his own beloved home he thinks,
And on the loved ones gathered round his hearth;
For them he utters many a fervent prayer,
And more and more his heart o'erflows with love.
And he is recompensed for all the toil
He underwent that he might hither come.
With him I kneel in prayer before thy throne,
Oh heavenly Virgin, and before thy Son.

The Pilgrim's return home.

Who is it wakes him out of heavenly sleep?
E'en now sweet morning lifts her veil from dawn.
With songs of joy the youthful day comes forth,
And hails the flying moon with smiling scorn.
With roseate hues the snow-clad alps are flushed.
The little bell rings out for holy Mass;
The temple's lofty doors are opened wide,
Already throng therein the pilgrim bands.

They come with staves held ready in their hands,
With garments girded for the journey back;
They come to offer Thee a farewell prayer
Oh Queen august, then to the stony paths
Which lead them home, they slowly bend their steps,
There to resume afresh their wonted life.
With sorrowing tears they tear themselves away,
So dear the spot has to their hearts become.

The Pilgrim goes, and from the farthest spot
Whence he the Sanctuary can still perceive,
Sends once more thither greetings and farewells.
Full happy does he deem the holy monks
Who rest have found within its quiet gates,
And aye the Mother blest and Child enjoy.
Go on thy way, oh pilgrim, know to all
Alike is life but one great pilgrimage.

Memories of Einsiedeln.

To silence hushed will be my songs by time,
And by his whirlwinds sweeping thro' the years.
And what I sang in freshness of my youth
In other hearts will seldom echo find.
Untwined will be the garland which I wove;
But still the theme I sang for aye will live.
Einsiedeln! ne'er will it forgotten be
In dazzling splendour it will ever shine.

Its walls indeed may into ruins fall;
The marble Chapel know its place no more;
The vaulted roofs and towers may all be riven;
And one by one extinguished be the lamps,

The birds of night may utter mournful plaints
Winging their flight from out the desert halls;
Perchance a wanderer, on some coming day,
May hither stray and o'er the ruins weep.

And yet Einsiedeln ever will remain;
The Einsiedeln which belongs not to this earth,
The heavenly spirit ever circling all.
Within this holy place, devotion's light,
That everlasting light which never fades,
But shines e'en though the earthly house decay.
Flames may indeed destroy material things
But, Phenix-like, the spirit from them springs.

CONTENTS.

Charles & Nioholas Benziger Brothers edit over 300 books of devotion, of which the following first three are English.

Short Prayers for little oatholics. With 1 engraving. Small in-32. 192 pages. Cover No. 2, cloth, gilt edges: 9d. ? -. 8, imitation cloth, gilt edges: 6d.

The little Path to Heaven. With 1 engraving. Small in-32. 288 pages. Cover No. 2, cloth, gilt edges: 1s. 1d. No. 11, imitation morocco, gilt edges: 1s. 3d.

Bible History containing the most remarkable events of the Old and New Testament, prepared for the use of the Catholic Schools. With 140 illustrations. In-8. 352 pages. Strong cardboard sides with cloth back, net. 1s.

The „Alte und Neue Welt", a fortnightly review, is the oldest and first in rank among the german catholic illustrated magazines.

The „*Alte und Neue Welt*", written for persons of every age and rank, always treats of subjects calculated to interest and amuse, without ever being offensive to the morals or hurtful to the mind. This review comprises all kinds of writings, and satisfies the desire for general knowledge which is so universal. Illustrated poems, tales, history, modern enterprises, inventions, discoveries, biographies of great men with faithful portraits etc., are all treated of in a most interesting manner.

The „*Alte und Neue Welt*" is rendered much more valuable owing to its being illustrated by numerous first-class artists. Special pains are taken with these illustrations which are really very true and life-like. It is needless to say that these are selected with as much care as the articles, for we are particularly careful to let nothing offensive enter our paper.

Owing to the lowness of its price and its real merit, it has now thousands of subscribers all over the world

The annual subscription, including postage and a very fine chromo as supplement, is 8s. 10d.

As we have in stock a small quantity of numbers of the past years, we are enabled to offer the public complete handsome volumes at the following reduced prices:

					s.	d.
Year 1867 to 1874 inclusive,	paper bound	. . . . .	3.	3
„ „ to „ „	handsomely bound in cloth	.	4.	10
„ 1875 to 1881 „	paper bound	. . . . .	4.	10
„ „ to „ „	handsomely bound in cloth	.	6.	5
„ 1882 to 1883 „	paper bound	. . . . .	6.	—
„ „ to „ „	handsomely bound in cloth	.	7.	8

www.ingramcontent.com/pod-product-compliance
Lightning Source LLC
Chambersburg PA
CBHW031058280326
41928CB00049B/969